Statistical Power Analysis
A Simple and General Model
for Traditional and Modern Hypothesis Tests

✦◆✦

Kevin R. Murphy
Colorado State University

Brett Myors
Macquarie University

LAWRENCE ERLBAUM ASSOCIATES, PUBLISHERS
1998   Mahwah, New Jersey   London

Lawrence Erlbaum Associates, Inc., Publishers
10 Industrial Avenue
Mahwah, New Jersey 07430

Cover Design by Kathryn Houghtaling Lacey

Library of Congress Cataloging-in-Publication Data

Murphy, Kevin R.,
Statistical power analysis : a simple and general model for
traditional and modern hypothesis testes / Kevin R. Murphy, Brett Myors
    p. cm.
Includes bibliographical references and index.
ISBN 0-8058-2946-6 (cloth : alk. paper). --ISBN 0-
8058-2947-4 (paper : alk. paper)
1. Statistical hypothesis testing. I. Myors, Brett. II
Title.
QA277.M87 1998
519.5'6--dc21

                                                    97-43919
                                                    CIP

Printed in the United States of America
10   9   8   7   6   5   4   3   2

Contents

Preface

One of the most common statistical procedures in the behavioral and social sciences is to test the hypothesis that treatments or interventions have no effect, or that the correlation between two variables is equal to zero, and so on (i.e., tests of the null hypothesis). Researchers have long been concerned with the possibility that they will reject the null hypothesis when it is in fact correct (i.e., make a Type I error), and an extensive body of research and data-analytic methods exists to help understand and control these errors. Substantially less attention has been devoted to the possibility that researchers will fail to reject the null hypothesis when in fact treatments, interventions, and so forth, have some real effect (i.e., make a Type II error). Statistical tests that fail to detect the real effects of treatments or interventions might substantially impede the progress of scientific research.

The statistical power of a test is the probability that it will lead researchers to reject the null hypothesis when that hypothesis is in fact wrong. Because most statistical tests are done in contexts where treatments have at least some effect (although it might be minuscule), power often translates into the probability that the test will lead to a correct conclusion about the null hypothesis. Viewed in this light, it is obvious why researchers have become interested in the topic of statistical power, and in methods of assessing and increasing the power of their tests.

This book presents a simple and general model for statistical power analysis based on the widely used F statistic. A wide variety of statistics used in the social and behavioral sciences can be thought of as specialized applications. The model for power analysis laid out here is quite simple, and it illustrates how these analyses work and how they can be applied to problems of study design, to evaluating others' research, and even to problems such as choosing the appropriate criterion for defining "statistically significant" outcomes.

In response to criticisms of traditional null hypothesis testing, several researchers have developed methods for testing what is referred to as "minimum-effect" hypotheses (i.e., the hypothesis that the effect of treatments, interventions, etc. exceeds some specific minimal level). This is the first book to discuss in detail the application of power analysis to both traditional null hypothesis tests and to minimum-effect tests. It shows how the same basic model applies to both types of testing, and illustrates applications of power analysis to both traditional null hypothesis tests (i.e., tests of the hypothesis that treatments have no effect) and to minimum-effect tests (i.e., tests of the hypothesis that the effects of treatments exceeds some minimal level). A single table is used to conduct both significance tests and power analyses for traditional and for minimum-effect tests (the "One-Stop F Table," presented in Appendix B), and it is explained how some relatively simple procedures allow researchers to ask a series of important and sophisticated questions about their research.

This book is intended for a wide audience, and therefore the presentations have been kept simple and nontechnical wherever possible. For example, Appendix A presents some fairly daunting statistical formulas, but it also shows how researchers with little expertise or interest in statistical analysis could quickly obtain the values needed to carry out power analyses for any range of hypotheses. Similarly, the first three chapters present a few formulas, but readers who skip them entirely will still be able to follow the ideas being presented.

Finally, most of the examples presented are drawn from the social and behavioral sciences, as are many of the generalizations about statistical methods that are most likely to be used. In part, this reflects our biases (as psychologists), but it also reflects the fact that issues related to power analysis have been widely discussed in this literature over the last several years. Researchers in other areas may find that some of the specific advice offered here does not apply as well to them, but the general principles articulated here will prove useful to researchers in a wide range of disciplines.

1

The Power of Statistical Tests

In the social and behavioral sciences, statistics serve two general purposes. First, they can be used to describe what happened in a particular study (*descriptive* statistics). Second, they can be used to help draw conclusions about what those results mean in some broader context (*inferential* statistics). The principal question in inferential statistics is whether an outcome, finding, or observation from a study reflects some underlying phenomenon in the population. For example, if 100 college sophomores are surveyed and it is determined that a majority prefer pizza to hot dogs, then does this mean that people in general (or college students in general) also prefer pizza? If a medical treatment yields improvements in 6 of 10 patients, does this mean it is an effective treatment that should be approved for general use?

The process of drawing inferences about populations from samples is a risky one, and a great deal has been written about the causes and cures for errors in statistical inference. Statistical power analysis (J. Cohen, 1988; Kraemer & Thiemann, 1987; Lipsey, 1990) falls under this general heading. Studies with too little statistical power can frequently lead to erroneous conclusions. In particular, they will very often lead to the incorrect conclusion that findings reported in a particular study are not likely to be true in a broader population. In the example cited earlier, the fact that a medical treatment worked for 6 of 10 patients is probably insufficient evidence that it is truly safe and effective, and if there is nothing more than this study to rely on, it might be concluded that the treatment has not been proven effective.

This conclusion may say as much about the low level of statistical power in the study as it does about the value of the treatment.

This chapter describes the rationale and applications of statistical power analysis. Most examples describe or apply power analysis in studies that assess the effect of some treatment or intervention (e.g., psychotherapy, reading instruction, performance incentives) by comparing outcomes for those who have received the treatment to outcomes of those who have not (nontreatment or control group). However, as is emphasized throughout this book, power analysis is applicable to a very wide range of statistical tests, and the same simple and general model can be applied to many of the statistical techniques used in the social and behavioral sciences.

THE STRUCTURE OF STATISTICAL TESTS

An understanding of statistical power first requires understanding the ideas that underlie statistical hypothesis testing. Suppose 50 children are exposed to a new method of reading instruction, which shows that their performance on reading tests is, on average, 6 points higher (on a 100-point test) than that of 50 similar children who received standard methods of instruction. Does this mean the new method is truly better? A 6-point difference might mean that the new method is really better, but it is also possible that there is no real difference between the two methods. This observed difference could be the result of the sort of random fluctuation that might be expected when the results are used from a single sample (here, the 100 children assigned to the two reading programs) to draw inferences about the effects of these two methods of instruction in the population.

One of the most basic ideas in statistical analysis is that results obtained in a sample do not necessarily reflect the state of affairs in the population from which that sample was drawn. For example, the fact that scores averaged six points higher in this particular group of children does not necessarily mean that scores are six points higher in the population, or that the same six-point difference would be found in another study examining a new group of students. Because samples do not (in general) perfectly represent the populations from which they were drawn, some instability should be expected in the results obtained from each sample. This instability is usually referred to as *sampling error*. One of the key goals of statistical theory is to estimate the amount of sampling error that is likely to be present in different statistical procedures and tests.

Statistical significance tests can be thought of as *decision aids*. That is, these tests can help researchers draw conclusions about whether the findings of a particular study represent real population effects, or whether they fall within the range of outcomes that might be produced by random sampling error. For example, there are two possible interpretations of the findings in this study of reading instruction: (a) the difference in average scores from the two programs is so small that it might reasonably represent nothing more than sampling error, or (b) the difference in average scores from the two programs is so large that it cannot be reasonably explained in terms of sampling error.

The most common statistical procedure in the social and behavioral sciences is to pit a *null* hypothesis (H_0) against an *alternative* hypothesis (H_1). In this example, the null and alternative hypotheses might take the following forms:

H_0—In the population, there is no difference in the average scores of those receiving these two methods of reading instruction.
H_1—In the population, there is a difference in the average scores of those receiving these two methods of reading instruction.

Although null hypotheses usually refer to "no difference" or "no effect," it is important to understand that there is nothing magic about the hypothesis that the difference between two groups is zero. It might be perfectly reasonable to evaluate the following set of possibilities:

H_0—In the population, the difference in the average scores of those receiving these two methods of reading instruction is six points.
H_1—In the population, the difference in the average scores of those receiving these two methods of reading instruction is not six points.

The null hypothesis (H_0) is a *specific* statement about results in a population that can be tested (and therefore nullified). One reason that null hypotheses are often framed in terms of "no effect" is that the alternative that is implied by this hypothesis is easy to interpret. If researchers test and reject the hypothesis that treatments have no effect, they are left with the alternative that treatments have at least some effect. Another reason for testing the hypothesis that treatments have no effect whatsoever is that probabilities, test statistics, and so on are easy to calculate when the effect of treatments is assumed to be nil.

In contrast, if researchers test and reject the hypothesis that the difference between treatments is exactly 6 points, they are left with a wide range of alternatives (e.g., the difference is 5 points, the difference is 10 points), including the possibility that there is no difference whatsoever. Although the hypothesis that treatments have no effect is the most common basis for statistical hypothesis tests (J. Cohen, 1994, refers to this as the "nil hypothesis"), as is shown later, there are a number of advantages to posing and testing substantive hypotheses about the size of treatment effects (Murphy & Myors, 1997). For example, it is easy to test the hypothesis that the effects of treatments are negligibly small (e.g., they account for 1% or less of the variance in outcomes). If this hypothesis is tested and rejected, the researcher is left with the alternative hypothesis that the effect of treatments is not trivially small, but rather is large enough to deserve at least some attention. The methods of power analysis described here are easily extended to such minimum-effect tests, and are not in any way limited to traditional tests of the null hypothesis that treatments have no effect.

What Determines the Outcomes of Statistical Tests?

There are four outcomes that can occur when the results obtained in a particular sample (e.g., the finding that one treatment works better than another in that sample) are used to draw inferences about a population (e.g., the inference that the treatment will also be better in the population). These outcomes are shown in Fig. 1.1.

The concern here is with understanding and minimizing errors in statistical inference; as Fig. 1.1 shows, there are two ways to make errors when testing hypotheses. First, it is possible that the treatment (e.g., new method of instruction) has no real effect in the population, but the results in the sample might lead to the belief that it does have some effect. If the results of this study were used to conclude that the new method of instruction was truly superior to the standard method, when in fact there were no differences, then this would be a *Type I* error. Type I errors might lead to wasting time and resources by pursuing what is essentially a dead end, and researchers have traditionally gone to great lengths to avoid these errors.

There is extensive literature dealing with methods of estimating and minimizing the occurrence of Type I errors (Zwick & Marascuilo, 1984). The probability of making a Type I error is in part a function of the standard or decision criterion used in testing a hypothesis (often referred to as alpha, or α). A very lenient standard (e.g., if there is any difference in the two samples, it will be concluded that there is also a difference in the population) might lead to more frequent Type I errors, whereas a more stringent standard might lead to few Type I errors.[1]

---

[1]It is important to note that Type I errors can only occur when there is no true treatment effect (i.e., when the null hypothesis is true), which is rarely the case. As a result, Type I errors are probably quite rare, and efforts to control these errors at the expense of making more Type II errors might be ill advised (Murphy, 1990).

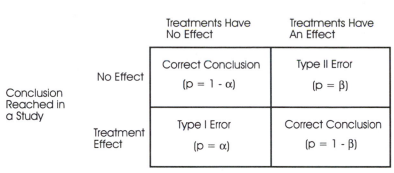

What is True in the Population?

	Treatments Have No Effect	Treatments Have An Effect
No Effect	Correct Conclusion $(p = 1 - \alpha)$	Type II Error $(p = \beta)$
Treatment Effect	Type I Error $(p = \alpha)$	Correct Conclusion $(p = 1 - \beta)$

Conclusion Reached in a Study

FIG. 1.1. Outcomes of statistical tests.

A second type of error referred to as *Type II* error, is common in statistical hypothesis testing (J. Cohen, 1994; Sedlmeier & Gigerenzer, 1989). A Type II error occurs when it is concluded that there is no treatment effect in the population, when in fact there is a real effect. Statistical power analysis is concerned with Type II errors. The power of a statistical test is defined as one minus the probability of making a Type II error (i.e., if the probability of making a Type II error is β, power = $1 - \beta$, or power is the probability that you will avoid a Type II error will be avoided). Studies with high levels of statistical power will rarely fail to detect the effects of treatments. If it is assumed that most treatments have at least some effect, then the statistical power of a study translates into the probability that the study will lead to the correct conclusion (i.e, that it will detect the effects of treatments).

Effects of Sensitivity, Effect Size, and Decision Criteria on Power

The power of a statistical test is a function of its sensitivity, the size of the effect in the population, and the standards or criteria used to test statistical hypotheses. Studies have higher levels of statistical power under the following conditions:

1. Studies are highly sensitive. Researchers might increase sensitivity by using better measures, or a study design that allows them to control for unwanted sources of variability in their data (for the moment, *sensitivity* is defined in terms of the degree to which sampling error introduces imprecision into the results of a study; a fuller definition is presented later). The simplest method of increasing the sensitivity of a study is to increase the sample size (N). As N increases, statistical estimates become more precise and the power of statistical tests increases.

2. Effect sizes (ES) are large. Different treatments have different effects. It is easiest to detect the effect of a treatment if that effect is large (e.g., when treatments account for a substantial proportion of variance in outcomes; specific measures of effect size are discussed later in this chapter and in the chapters that follow). When treatments have very small effects, these effects can be difficult to reliably detect. Power increases as ES values increase.
3. Standards are set that make it easier to reject H_0. It is easier to reject H_0 when the significance criterion, or alpha (α) level, is .05 than when it is .01 or .001. Power increases as the standard for determining significance becomes more lenient.

Power is highest when all three of these conditions are met (i.e., sensitive study, large effect, lenient criterion for rejecting the null hypothesis). In practice, sample size (which affects sensitivity) is probably the most important determinant of power. Effect sizes in the social and behavioral sciences tend to be small or moderate (if the effect of a treatment is so large that it can be detected even in small samples, then there may be little reason to test for the effect), and researchers are often unwilling to abandon the traditional criteria for statistical significance that are accepted in their field (usually, alpha levels of .05 or .01; Cowles & Davis, 1982). Thus, effect sizes and decision criteria tend to be similar across a wide range of studies. In contrast, sample sizes vary considerably, and they directly impact levels of power. With a sufficiently large N, virtually any statistic will be *significantly* different from zero, and virtually any null hypothesis that is tested will be rejected. Large N makes statistical tests highly sensitive, and virtually any specific point hypothesis can be rejected if the study is *sufficiently sensitive* (as is shown later, this is not true for tests of the hypothesis that treatment effects fall in some range of values defined as *negligibly small* or *meaningfully large*). For example, if the effect of a new medication is an increase of .0000001% in the success rate of treatments, then the null hypothesis that treatments have no effect is formally wrong, and will be rejected in a study that is sufficiently sensitive. With a small enough N, researchers may not have enough power to reliably detect the effects of even the most substantial treatments.

Studies can have very low levels of power (i.e., are likely to make Type II errors) when they use small samples, when the effect being studied is a small one, and/or when stringent criteria are used to define a significant result. The worst case occurs when researchers use a small sample to study a treatment that has a very small effect, and they use a very strict standard for rejecting the null hypothesis. Under those conditions, Type II errors may be the norm. To put it simply, studies that use small samples and stringent criteria for statistical significance to examine treatments that are likely to have small effects will almost always lead to the wrong conclusion about those treatments.

THE MECHANICS OF POWER ANALYSIS

When a sample is drawn from a population, the exact value of any statistic (e.g., the mean, difference between two group means) is uncertain, and that uncertainty is reflected by a statistical distribution. If a treatment is introduced that has no real effect, researchers will not always find that the two groups have exactly the same scores. Rather, there is some range of values they might expect for any test statistic in a study like this, and the standards used to determine statistical significance are based on this range or distribution of values. In traditional null hypothesis testing, a test statistic is *statistically significant* at the .05 level if its actual value is outside of the range of values that would be observed 95% of the time in studies where the treatment had no real effect. If the test statistic is outside of this range, the inference is that the treatment did have some real effect.

For example, suppose that 62 people are randomly assigned to treatment and control groups, and the *t* statistic is used to compare the means of the two groups. If the treatment has no effect whatsoever, the *t* statistic should usually be near zero, and will have a value less than or equal to 2.00 in 95% of all such studies. If the *t* statistic obtained in a study is larger than 2.00, it may be inferred that treatments are very likely to have some effect; if there was no real effect of treatments, values above 2.00 would be a very rare event.

As the previous example suggests, if treatments have no effect whatsoever in the population, then researchers should not expect to always find a difference of precisely zero between samples of those who do and do not receive the treatment. Rather, there is some range of values that might be found for any test statistic in a sample (e.g., in the example cited earlier, the value of a *t* statistic is expected to be near zero, but it is also known that it might range from -2.00 to +2.00). The same is true if treatments have a real effect. For example, if researchers expect that the mean in a treatment group will be 10 points higher than the mean in the nontreatment group (e.g., because this is the size of the difference in the population), they should also expect some variability around that figure. Sometimes, the difference might be 9 points, and sometimes it might be 11 or 12 points. The key to power analysis is estimating the range of values that might reasonably be expected for some statistic if the real effect of treatments is small, medium, or large.

Figure 1.2 illustrates the key ideas in statistical power analysis. Suppose researchers devise a new test statistic and use it to evaluate the six-point difference in reading test scores described earlier. The larger the difference between the two treatment groups, the larger the value of the test statistic. To be statistically significant, the value of this test statistic must be 2.00 or larger. As Fig. 1.2 suggests, the chance researchers will reject the null hypothesis that there is no difference between the two groups depends substantially on whether the true effect of treatments is small or large.

If the null hypothesis that there is no real effect was true, they would expect to find values of 2.00 or higher for this test statistic in 5 tests out of every 100 performed (i.e., " = .05). This is illustrated in section 1 of Fig. 1.2. Section 2 of Fig. 1.2 illustrates the distribution of test statistic values researchers might expect if treatments had a small effect on the

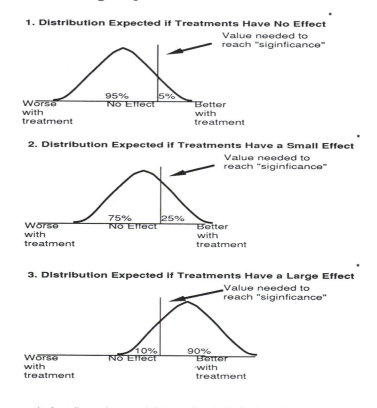

* - depending on the test statistic in question, the distributions might take different forms, but the essential features of this figure would apply to any test statistic

FIG. 1.2. Essentials of power analysis.

dependent variable. They might notice that the distribution of test statistics they would expect to find in studies of a treatment with this sort of effect has shifted a bit, and in this case 25% of the values they might expect to find are greater than or equal to 2.00. That is, if researchers run a study under the scenario illustrated in section 2 of Fig. 1.2 (i.e., treatments have a small effect), the probability they will reject the null hypothesis is .25. Section 3 of Fig. 1.2 illustrates the distribution of values they might expect if the true effect of treatments is large. In this distribution, 90% of the values are 2.00 or greater, and the probability they will reject the null hypothesis is .90. The power of a statistical test is the proportion of the distribution of test statistics expected for that study that is above the critical value used to establish statistical significance.

No matter what hypothesis is being tested, or what statistic is being used to test that hypothesis, power analysis always involves three basic steps, which are listed in Table 1.1. First, researchers must set some criterion or critical value for statistical significance. For example, the tables found in the back of virtually any statistics textbook can be used to determine such critical values for testing the traditional null hypothesis. If the test statistic computed exceeds this critical value, then the null will be rejected. However, these tables are not the only basis for setting such a criterion. Suppose researchers want to test the hypothesis that the effects of treatments are so small that they can safely be ignored. This might involve specifying some range of effects that would be designated as "negligible," and then determining the critical value of a statistic needed to reject this hypothesis. Chapter 2 shows how such tests are done, and the implications of such hypothesis testing strategies for statistical power analysis.

TABLE 1.1

The Three Steps to Determining Statistical Power

1. Establish a criterion or critical value for statistical significance.
   * What is the hypothesis (e.g. traditional null hypothesis, minimum-effect test)
   * What level of confidence is desired (e.g. $\alpha = .05$, $\alpha = .01$)
   * What is the critical value for the test statistic (based on the chosen H_0 and α)?

2. Estimate the effect size.
   * Are the treatments expected to have a large, medium, or small effect
   * What is the range of values expected for the test statistic, given this effect size

3. Determine where the critical value lies in relation to the distribution of test statistics that are expected in a study.
   * The power of a statistical test is the proportion of the distribution of test statistics expected for that study that is above the critical value used to establish statistical significance.

Second, an effect size must be estimated. That is, researchers must make their best guess of how much effect the treatments being studied are likely to have on the dependent variable(s) of interest; methods of estimating Table 1.1 effect sizes are discussed later in this chapter. As noted earlier, if there are good reasons to believe that treatments have a very large effect, it should be quite easy to reject the null hypothesis. On the other hand, if the true effects of treatments are small and subtle, it might be very hard to reject the hypothesis that they have no real effect.

Once the effect size has been estimated, it is also possible to use that estimate to describe the distribution of test statistics researchers should expect to find in studies of that particular treatment or set of treatments. This process is described in more detail in chapter 2, but a simple example serves to illustrate. Suppose researchers are using the t test to assess the difference in the mean scores of those receiving two different treatments. If there was no real difference between the treatments, they would expect to find t values near zero most of the time, and they could use statistical theory to tell how much they might depart from zero as a result of sampling error. The t tables in most statistics textbooks tell how much variability they might expect with samples of different sizes, and once they know the mean (here, zero) and the standard deviation of this distribution, it is easy to estimate what proportion of the distribution falls above or below any critical value. If there is a large difference between the treatments (e.g., the dependent variable has a mean of 500 and a standard deviation of 100, and the mean for one treatment is usually 80 points higher than the mean for another), then they should expect to find large t values most of the time. Once again, statistical theory can be used to estimate the distribution of values that would be expected in such studies.

The final step in power analysis is a comparison between the values obtained in the first two steps. For example, if researchers determine that they need a t value of 2.00 to reject a particular null hypothesis, and they also determine that because the treatments being studied have very large effects they are likely to find t values of 2.00 or greater 90% of the time, then they have also determined the power of this test - (i.e., power is .90).

Sensitivity and Power

Sensitivity refers to the precision with which a statistical test distinguishes between true treatment effects and differences in scores that are the result of sampling error. As already noted, the sensitivity of statistical tests is largely a function of the sample size. Large samples

TABLE 1.2
Examples of Effect Sizes Reported in Lipsey and Wilson (1993) Review

Effect Size	Dependent Variable	d
Small (d = .20)		
Treatment programs for juvenile delinquents	delinquency outcomes	.17
Worksite smoking cessation/reduction programs	quit rates	.21
Small vs. large class size, all grade levels	achievement measures	.20
Medium (d = .50)		
Behavior therapy vs. placebo controls	various outcomes	.51
Chronic disease patient education	compliance and health	.52
Enrichment programs for gifted children	cognitive, creativity, affective outcomes	.55
Large (d = .80)		
Psychotherapy	various outcomes	.85
Meditation and relaxation techniques	blood pressure	.93
Positive reinforcement in the classroom	learning	1.17

provide very precise estimates of population parameters, whereas small samples produce results that can be unstable and untrustworthy. For example, if 6 in 10 children do better with a new reading curriculum than with the old one, then this might reflect nothing more than simple sampling error. If 600 of 1,000 children do better with the new curriculum, then this is powerful and convincing evidence that there are real differences between the new and the old curriculum. In a study with low sensitivity, there is considerable uncertainty about statistical outcomes. As a result, it might be possible to find a large treatment effect in a sample, even though there is no true treatment effect in the population. This translates into substantial variability in study outcomes, and the need for relatively demanding tests of statistical significance. If outcomes can vary substantially from study to study, researchers need to observe a relatively large effect to be confident that it represents a true treatment effect and not merely sampling error. As a result, it will be difficult to reject the hypothesis that there is no true effect, and many Type II errors might be made.

In a highly sensitive study, there is very little uncertainty or random variation in study outcomes, and virtually any difference between treatment and control groups is likely to be accepted as an indication that the treatment has an effect in the population.

Effect Size and Power

Effect size is a key concept in statistical power analysis (J. Cohen, 1988; Rosenthal, 1991; Tatsuoka, 1993a). At the simplest level, *effect size measures* provide a standardized index of how much impact treatments actually have on the dependent variable. One of the most common effect size measures is the standardized mean difference, d, defined as $d = (M_t - M_c)/SD$, where M_t and M_c are the treatment and control group means, respectively, and SD is the pooled standard deviation. By expressing the difference in group means in standard deviation units, the d statistic provides a simple metric that allows researchers to compare treatment effects from different studies, areas or research, and so on, without having to keep track of the units of measurement used in different studies or areas of research. For example, Lipsey and Wilson (1993) cataloged the effects of a wide range of psychological, educational, and behavioral treatments, all expressed in terms of d. Examples of interventions in these areas that have relatively small, moderately large, and large effects on specific sets of outcomes are presented in Table 1.2.

For example, worksite smoking cessation/reduction programs have a relatively small effect on quit rates ($d = .21$). The effects of class size on achievement or of juvenile delinquency programs on delinquency outcomes are similarly small. Concretely, a d value of .20 means that the difference between the average score of those who do and do not receive the treatment is only 20% as large as the standard deviation of the outcome measure within each of the treatment groups. This standard deviation measures the variability in outcomes, independent of treatments, so $d = .20$ indicates that the average effect of treatments is only one fifth as large as the variability in outcomes that might occur with no treatments. In contrast, interventions such as psychotherapy, meditation and relaxation, or positive reinforcement in the classroom have relatively large effects on outcomes such as functioning levels, blood pressure, and learning (d values range from .85 to 1.17).

As Fig. 1.2 suggests, when the true treatment effect is very small, it might be hard to accurately and consistently detect this effect in study samples. For example, aspirin can be useful in reducing heart attacks, but the effects are relatively small ($d = .068$; see, however, Rosenthal, 1993). As a result, studies of 20 or 30 patients taking aspirin or a placebo will not consistently detect the true and life-saving effects of this drug. Large sample studies, however, provide compelling evidence of the consistent effect of aspirin on heart attacks. On the other hand, if the effect is relatively large, it is easy to detect, even with a relatively small sample. For example, cognitive ability has a strong influence on performance in school (d is about 1.10), and the effects of individual differences in cognitive ability are readily noticeable even in small samples of students.

Decision Criteria and Power

Finally, the standard or decision criteria used in hypothesis testing has a critical impact on statistical power. The standards used to test statistical hypotheses are usually set with a goal of minimizing Type I errors; alpha levels are usually set at .05, .01, or some other similarly low level, reflecting a strong bias against treating study outcomes that might be due to nothing more than sampling error as meaningful (Cowles & Davis, 1982). Setting a more lenient standard makes it easier to reject the null hypothesis, and whereas this can lead to Type I errors in those rare cases where the null is actually true, anything that makes it easier to reject the null hypothesis also increases the statistical power of the study.

As Fig. 1.1 shows, there is always a tradeoff between Type I and Type II errors. If researchers make it very difficult to reject the null hypothesis, they will minimize Type I errors (incorrect rejections), but will also increase the number of Type II errors. That is, if they rarely reject the null, they will often incorrectly dismiss sample results as mere sampling error, when the results may in fact indicate the true effects of treatments. Numerous authors have noted that procedures to control or minimize Type I errors can substantially reduce statistical power, and may cause more problems (i.e., Type II errors) than they solve (J. Cohen, 1994; Sedlmeier & Gigerenzer, 1989).

Power Analysis and the General Linear Model

The chapters that follow describe a simple and general model for statistical power analysis. This model is based on the widely used F statistic. This statistic (and variations on the F) is used to test a wide range of statistical hypotheses in the context of the general linear model (J. Cohen & P. Cohen, 1983; Horton, 1978; Tatsuoka, 1993b), which provides the basis for correlation, multiple regression, analysis of variance, descriptive discriminant analysis, and all of the variations of these techniques. The general linear model subsumes a large proportion of the statistics that are widely used in the social sciences, and by tying statistical power analysis to this model, it can be shown how the same simple set of techniques can be applied to an extraordinary range of statistical analyses.

STATISTICAL POWER OF RESEARCH
IN THE SOCIAL AND BEHAVIORAL SCIENCES

Research in the social and behavioral science often shows shockingly low levels of power. Starting with J. Cohen's (1962) review, studies in psychology, education, communication, journalism, and other related fields have routinely documented power in the range of .20 to .50 for detecting small to medium treatment effects (Sedlmeier & Gigerenzer, 1989). In other words, it is typical for studies in these areas to have a 20% to 50% chance of rejecting the null hypothesis. If it is to be believed that the null hypothesis is virtually always wrong (i.e., that treatments have at least some effect, even if it is a very small one), this means that at least half of the studies, and perhaps as many as 80% of the studies in these areas, are likely to reach the wrong conclusion when testing the null hypothesis. This is even more startling and discouraging when considering that these reviews have examined the statistical power of published research. Given the strong biases against publishing methodologically suspect studies or studies reporting null results, it is likely that the studies that survive the editorial review process are better than the norm, that they show stronger effects than similar unpublished studies, and that the statistical power of unpublished studies is even lower.

Studies that do not reject the null hypothesis are often regarded by researchers as failures. The levels of power reported earlier suggest that "failure," defined in these terms, is quite common. If a treatment effect is small, and researchers design a study with a power level of .20 (which is depressingly typical), they are four times as likely to fail (i.e., fail to reject the null) as to succeed. Power of .50 suggests that the outcome of the study is basically like the flip of a coin. They are just as likely to fail as they are to succeed. It is likely that much of the apparent inconsistency in research findings is due to nothing more than inadequate power (Schmidt, 1992). If 100 studies are conducted, each with power of .50, half of them will reject the null and half will not. Given the stark implications of low power, it is important to consider why research in the social and behavioral sciences is so often conducted in a way in which failure is more likely than success.

The most obvious possibility is that social scientists tend to study treatments, interventions, and so on. that have very small and unreliable effects. Until recently, this explanation was widely accepted, but the widespread use of metanalysis in integrating scientific literature suggests that this is not the case. There is now ample evidence from literally hundreds of analyses of thousands of individual studies that the treatments, interventions, and the like studied by behavioral and social scientists have substantial and meaningful effects (Haase, Waechter, & Solomon, 1982; J. E. Hunter & Hirsh, 1987; Lipsey, 1990; Lipsey & Wilson, 1993; Schmitt, Gooding, Noe, & Kirsch, 1984); these effects are of a similar order of magnitude as many of the effects reported in the physical sciences (Hedges, 1987). A second possibility is that the decision criteria used to define statistical significance are too stringent. It is argued in several of the following chapters that researchers are often too concerned with Type I errors and insufficiently concerned with statistical power. However, the use of overly stringent decision criteria is probably not the best explanation for low levels of statistical power.

The best explanation for the low levels of power observed in many areas of research is many studies use samples that are much too small to provide accurate and credible results. Researchers routinely use samples of 20, 50, or 75 observations to make inferences about population parameters. When sample results are unreliable, it is necessary to set some strict standard to distinguish real treatment effects from fluctuations in the data that are due to simple sampling error, and studies with these small samples often fail to reject null hypotheses, even when the population treatment effect is fairly large. On the other hand, very large samples will allow the rejection of the null hypothesis even when it is very nearly true (i.e., when the effect of treatments is very small). In fact, the effects of sample size on statistical power are so profound that it is tempting to conclude that a significance test is little more than a roundabout measure of how large the sample is. If the sample is sufficiently small, then researchers will virtually never reject the null hypothesis. If the sample is sufficiently large, they will virtually always reject the null hypothesis.

USING POWER ANALYSIS

Statistical power analysis can be used for both planning and diagnosis. The most typical use of power analysis is in designing research studies. A power analysis can be used to determine how large the sample should be, or in deciding what criterion should be used to define statistical significance. Power analysis can also be used as a diagnostic tool, to determine whether a specific study has adequate power for specific purposes, or to identify the sort of effects that can be reliably detected in that study.

Because power is a function of the sensitivity of the study (which is essentially a function of N), the size of the effect in the population (ES), and the decision criterion used to determine statistical significance, researchers can solve for any of the four values (i.e., power, N, ES, α), given the other three. However, none of these values is necessarily known in advance, although some values may be set by convention. The criterion for statistical significance (i.e., α) is often set at .05 or .01 by convention, but there is nothing sacred about these values. As is noted later, one important use of power analysis is in making decisions about what criteria should be used to describe a result as significant.

The effect size depends on the treatment, phenomenon, or variable being studied, and is usually not known in advance. Sample size is rarely set in advance, and N often depends on some combination of luck and resources on the part of the investigator. Actual power levels are rarely known, and it can be difficult to obtain sensible advice about how much power to have in a study. It is important to understand how each of the parameters involved is determined when conducting a power analysis.

Determining the Effect Size

There is a built-in dilemma in power analysis. In order to determine the statistical power of a study, the effect size must be known. But if researchers already knew the exact strength of the effect the particular treatment, intervention, and so on, they would not need to do the study! The whole point of the study is to find out what effect the treatment has, and the true effect size in the population is unlikely to ever be known.

Statistical power analyses are always based on estimates of the effect size. In many areas of study, there is a substantial body of theory and empirical research that will provide a well-grounded estimate of the effect size. For example, there are literally hundreds of studies of the validity of cognitive ability tests as predictors of job performance (J. E. Hunter & Hirsch, 1987; Schmidt, 1992), and this literature suggests that the relation between test scores and performance is consistently strong (corrected correlations of about .50 are frequently seen). If researchers wanted to estimate the statistical power of a study of the validity of a cognitive ability test, they could use the results from this literature to estimate the effect size they expect to find. Even where there is not an extensive literature available, researchers can often use their experience with similar studies to realistically estimate effect sizes.

When there is no good basis for estimating effect sizes, power analyses can still be carried out by making a conservative estimate. A study that has adequate power to reliably detect small effects (e.g., a d of .20, a correlation of .10) will also have adequate power to detect larger effects. On the other hand, if researchers design studies with the assumption that effects will be large, they might have insufficient power to detect small but important effects. Earlier, it was noted that the effects of taking aspirin on heart attacks are relatively small, but there is still a substantial payoff for taking the drug. If the initial research that led to the use of aspirin for this purpose had been conducted using small samples, the researchers would have had little chance of detecting this life-saving effect.

Determining the Desired Level of Power

In determining desired levels of power, the researcher must weigh the risks of running studies without adequate power against the resources needed to attain high levels of power. High levels of power can always be achieved by using very large samples, but the time and expense required may not always justify the effort.

There are no hard-and-fast rules about how much power is enough, but there does seem to be consensus about two things. First, if at all possible, power should be above .50. When power drops below .50, the study is more likely to fail (i.e., it is unlikely to reject the null hypothesis) than succeed. It is hard to justify designing studies in which failure is the most likely outcome. Second, power of .80 or above is usually judged to be adequate. The .80 convention is arbitrary (in the same way that significance criteria of .05 or .01 are arbitrary), but it seems to be widely accepted, and it can be rationally defended.

Power of .80 means that success (rejecting the null) is four times as likely as failure. It can be argued that some number other than four might represent a more acceptable level of risk (e.g., if power = .90, success is nine times as likely as failure), but it is often prohibitively difficult to achieve power much in excess of .80. For example, to have a power of .80 in detecting a small treatment effect (where the difference between treatment and control groups is $d = .20$), a total sample of about 775 subjects is necessary. If researchers want power to be .95, they need about 1,300 subjects. Most power analyses specify .80 as the desired level of power to be achieved, and this convention seems to be widely accepted.

Applying Power Analysis

There are four ways researchers can use power analysis: in determining the sample size needed to achieve desired levels of power, in determining the level of power in a study that is planned or has already been conducted, in determining the size of effect that can be reliably detected by a particular study, and in determining sensible criteria for statistical significance. The chapters that follow will lay out the actual steps in doing a power analysis, but it is useful at this point to get a preview of the following four potential applications of this method:

1. Determining sample size. Given a particular ES, significance criterion and a desired level of power, it is easy to solve for the sample size needed. For example, if researchers think the correlation between a new test and performance on the job is .30, and they want to have at least an 80% chance of rejecting the null hypothesis (with a significance criterion of .05), they need a sample of about 80 cases. When planning a study, they should routinely use power analysis to help make sensible decisions about the number of subjects needed.
2. Determining power levels. If N, ES, and the criterion for statistical significance are known, researchers can use power analysis to determine the level of power for that study. For example, if the difference between treatment and control groups is small (e.g., $d = .20$), there are 50 subjects in each group, and the significance criterion in $\alpha = .01$, then power will be only .05! Researchers should certainly expect that this study will fail to reject the null, and they might decide to change the design of the research considerably (e.g., use larger samples, more lenient criteria).
3. Determine ES levels. Researchers can also determine what sort of effect could be reliably detected, given N, the desired level of power, and α. In the example cited, a study with 50 subjects in both the treatment and control groups would have power of .80 to detect a very large effect (approximately $d = .65$) with a .01 significance criterion, or a large effect ($d = .50$) with a .05 significance criterion.
4. Determine criteria for statistical significance. Given a specific effect, sample size, and power level, it is possible to determine the significance criterion. For example, if researchers expect a correlation coefficient to be .30, $N = 67$, and they want power to equal or exceed .80, they will need to use a significance criterion of $\alpha = .10$ rather than the more common .05 or .01.

CONCLUSIONS

Power is defined as the probability that a study will reject the null hypothesis when it is in fact false. Studies with high statistical power are very likely to detect the effects of treatments, interventions, and so on, whereas studies with low power will often lead researchers to dismiss potentially important effects as sampling error. The statistical power of a test is a function of the size of the treatment effect in the population, the sample size, and the particular criteria used to define statistical significance. Although most discussions of power analysis are phrased in terms of traditional null hypothesis testing, where the hypothesis that treatments have no impact whatsoever is tested, this technique can be fruitfully applied to any method of statistical hypothesis testing.

Statistical power analysis has received less attention in the behavioral and social sciences than it deserves. It is still routine in many areas to run studies with disastrously low levels of power. Statistical power analysis can be used to determine the number of subjects that should be included in a study, to estimate the likelihood that the study will reject the null hypothesis, to determine what sorts of effects can be reliably detected in a study, or to make rational decisions about the standards used to define statistical significance. Each of these applications of power analysis is taken up in the next chapters.

2
A Simple and General Model for Power Analysis

This chapter develops a simple approach to statistical power analysis based on the widely used F statistic. This statistic (or some transformation of F) is used to test statistical hypotheses in the *general linear model* (Horton, 1978; Tatsuoka, 1993b), which includes all of the variations of correlation and regression analysis (including multiple regression), analysis of variance and covariance (ANOVA and ANCOVA), t tests for differences in group means, tests of the hypothesis that the effect of treatments takes on a specific value, or a value different from zero. The great majority of the statistical tests that are used in the social and behavioral sciences can be treated as special cases of the general linear model.

This is not the only approach to statistical power analysis. For example, in the most comprehensive work on power analysis, J. Cohen (1988) constructed power tables for a wide range of statistics and statistical applications using separate effect size measures and power calculations for each class of statistics. Kraemer and Thiemann (1987) derived a general model for statistical power analysis based on the intraclass correlation coefficient, and developed methods for expressing a wide range of test statistics in terms that were compatible with a single general table based on the intraclass r. Lipsey (1990) used the t test as a basis for estimating the statistical power of several statistical tests.

WHY USE THE *F* DISTRIBUTION AS A BASIS FOR POWER ANALYSIS?

Basing a model for statistical power analysis on the *F* statistic provides an optimal balance between applicability and familiarity. First, the *F* statistic is ubiquitous. This chapter and the next, show how to transform a wide range of test statistics, along with several common effect size measures into *F* statistics, and how to use those *F* values in statistical power analysis. Because such a wide range of statistics can be transformed into *F* values, structuring power analysis around the *F* distribution allows researchers to cover a great deal of ground with a single set of tables.

Second, the approach developed here is flexible. Unlike other presentations of power analysis, this discussion does not limit itself to tests of the traditional null hypothesis (i.e, the hypothesis that treatments have no effect whatsoever). This particular type of test has been roundly criticized (J. Cohen, 1994; Meehl, 1978; Morrison & Henkel, 1970), and there is a need to move beyond such limited tests. The discussions of power analysis consider several methods of statistical hypothesis testing, and show how power analysis can be easily extended beyond the traditional framework in which the possibility that treatments have no effect whatsoever is tested. In particular, it is shown how the model developed here can be used to evaluate the power of *minimum-effect hypothesis* tests (i.e., tests of the hypothesis that the effects of treatments exceed some predetermined minimum level).

Recently, researchers have devoted considerable attention to alternatives to the traditional null hypothesis test (e.g., Murphy & Myors, 1997; Rouanet, 1996; Serlin & Lapsley, 1985, 1993), focusing in particular on tests of the hypothesis that the effect of treatments falls within or outside of some range of values. For example, Murphy and Myors (1997) discussed alternatives to tests of the traditional null hypothesis that involve specifying some range of effects that would be regarded as negligibly small, and then testing the hypothesis that the effect of treatments falls within this range (H_0) or falls above this range (H_1; i.e., the effects of treatments are so large that they cannot reasonably be described as negligible). The *F* statistic is particularly well-suited for such tests. This statistic ranges in value from zero to infinity, with larger values accompanying stronger effects. As is shown in the following sections, this property of the *F* statistic makes it easy to adapt familiar testing procedures to evaluate the hypothesis that effects exceed some minimum level, rather than simply evaluating the possibility that treatments have no effect at all.

Finally, the F distribution explicitly incorporates one of the key ideas of statistical power analysis (i.e., that the range of values that might be expected for a variety of test statistics depends in part on the size of the effect in the population). As is explained later, the notion of effect size is reflected very nicely by one of the three parameters that determines the distribution of the statistic F (i.e., the noncentrality parameter).

The General Linear Model, the F Statistic and Effect Size

Before exploring the F distribution and its use in power analysis, it is useful to briefly describe the key ideas in applying the general linear model as a method of structuring statistical analyses, show how the F statistic is used in testing hypotheses in this model, and describe a very general index of whether treatments, interventions, tests, and so on have large or small effects.

Suppose that 200 children are randomly assigned to one of two methods of reading instruction. Each child receives this instruction, either accompanied by audiovisual aids (e.g., computer software that "reads" to the child while showing pictures on a screen) or without the aids. At the end of the semester, each child's performance in reading is measured.

One way to structure research on the possible effects of reading instruction methods and/or audiovisual aids is to construct a model to explain why some children read well and others read poorly. This model might take the form:

$$y_{ijk} = \alpha_i + \beta_j + \alpha_{\beta ij} + e_{ijk} \tag{1}$$

where:

y_{ijk} = the score of child k, who received instruction method i and audiovisual aid j

α_i = the effect of the method of reading instruction

β_j = the effect of audiovisual aids

$\alpha_{\beta ij}$ = the effect of the interaction between method of instruction and audiovisual aids

e_{ijk} = the part of the children's score that cannot be explained by the treatments they received

In a linear model of this sort, researchers might reasonably ask several sorts of questions. First, it makes sense to ask whether the effect of a particular treatment or combination of treatments is large enough to allow researchers to rule out sampling error as an explanation for people receiving one treatment getting higher scores than people not receiving it. As is explained later, the F statistic is well suited for this purpose.

Second, it makes sense to ask whether the effects of treatments, interventions, and so on are relatively large or relatively small. There are a variety of statistics that might be used in answering this question, but one very general approach is to estimate the percentage of variance in scores (PV) that is explained by the various effects included in the model. Regardless of the specific approach taken in statistical testing under the general linear model (e.g., analysis of variance or covariance, multiple regression, t tests), the goal of the model is always to explain variance in the dependent variable (i.e., to help understand why some children obtained higher scores than others). General linear models divide the total variance in scores into that which can be explained by treatment effects (i.e., the combined effects of instruction methods and audiovisual aids) and that which cannot be explained in terms of the treatments received by subjects. The percentage of variance (PV) associated with each effect in a linear model provides one very general measure of whether treatment effects are large or small.

There are a number of specific statistics used in estimating PV, notably η^2 (eta squared) and R^2, which are typically encountered in the contexts of the analysis of variance and multiple regression, respectively. This chapter prefers the more general term PV, because it helps to keep in mind that is referring to a general index of the effects of treatments or interventions, not to any specific statistic or statistical approach. As is shown later, estimates of PV are extremely useful in structuring statistical power analyses for virtually any of the specific applications of the general linear model.

THE F DISTRIBUTION AND POWER

If researchers take the ratio of two independent estimates of the variance in a population (e.g., s^2_1 and s^2_2), this ratio is distributed as F, where:

$$F = s^2_1/s^2_2 \text{ , with degrees of freedom of v1 and v2} \qquad (2)$$

This F ratio can be used to test a wide range of statistical hypotheses (e.g., testing for the equality of means and variances). In the general linear model, the F statistic is used to test the null hypothesis (e.g., that the means are equal across treatments) by comparing some measure of the variability in scores due to the treatments to some measure of the variability in scores that might be expected as a result of simple sampling error. In its most general form, the F test in general linear models is:

$$F = \text{variability due to treatments/variability due to error}   (3)$$

The distribution of the statistic F is complex, and depends in part on both the degrees of freedom of the effect being tested (v1) and the degrees of freedom for the estimate of error used in the test (v2). If treatments have no effect whatsoever, the expected value of F is v2/(v2 - 2), which is very close to 1.0 for values of v2 much greater than 10. That is, if the traditional null hypothesis is true (i.e., treatments have no effect whatsoever), then researchers should expect to find F ratios of about 1.0. However, as already noted, they should also expect some variability in the F values actually obtained, even if the null hypothesis is literally true (because of sampling error). Depending on the degrees of freedom (v1 and v2), the F values they expect to find if the null hypothesis is true might cluster closely around 1.00, or they might vary considerably. The F tables shown in most statistics textbooks give a sense of how much these values might vary strictly as a function of sampling error, given various combinations of v1 and v2.

Finally, it is useful to note that the F and chi-squared distributions are closely related (the ratio of two chi-squared variables, each divided by its degrees of freedom, is distributed as F), and both distributions are special cases of a more general form (the gamma distribution).

The Noncentral F

Most familiar statistical tests are based on the central F distribution (i.e., the distribution of F statistics that should be expected when the traditional null hypothesis is true). However, as noted earlier, interventions or treatments normally have at least some effect, and the distribution of F values expected in any particular study is likely to take the form of a noncentral F distribution. The power of the statistical test is defined by the proportion of that noncentral distribution that exceeds the critical value used to define statistical significance. The shape and range of values in the noncentral F distribution is a function of both the degrees of freedom (v1 and v2) and the *noncentrality parameter* (λ). One way to think of the noncentrality parameter is as a function of just how wrong the traditional null hypothesis is. When $\lambda = 0$ (i.e., when the traditional null hypothesis is true), the noncentral F is identical to the central F that is tabled in most statistics texts.

The exact value of the noncentrality parameter is function of both the effect size and the sensitivity of the statistical test (which is largely a function of N). For example, in a study where n subjects are randomly assigned to each of four treatment conditions, $\lambda = (n\Sigma(\mu_j - \mu)^2)/\sigma^2_e$, where μ^j and μ represent the population mean in treatment group j and the population mean over all four treatments, and σ^2_e represents the variance in scores due to sampling error. Horton (1978) noted that in many *general linear model* applications:

$$\lambda_{est} = SS_{effect} / MS_e \qquad (4)$$

where λ_{est} represents an estimate of the noncentrality parameter, SS_{effect} represents the sum of squares for the effect of interest, and MS_e represents the mean square error term used to test hypotheses about that effect. Using PV to designate the proportion of the total variance in the dependent variable explained by treatments (which means that $1 - PV$ refers to the proportion not explained), it is possible to estimate the noncentrality parameter with the following equation:

$$\lambda_{est} = v2\ [PV/(1 - PV)] \qquad (5)$$

Equation 5 provides a practical method for estimating the value of the noncentrality parameter in virtually any application of the general linear model.[1]

The noncentrality parameter reflects the upward shift of the F distribution as the size of the effect in the population increases (Horton, 1978). For example, if N subjects are randomly assigned to one of k treatments, the mean of the noncentral F distribution is approximately $[((N - k)/(N - k - 2)) * (1 + \lambda/(k - 1))]$ as compared to an approximate mean of 1.0 for the central F distribution. More concretely, assume that 100 subjects are assigned to one of four treatments. If the null hypothesis is true, then the expected value of F is approximately 1.0. However, if the effect of treatments is in fact large (e.g., $PV = .25$), researchers should expect to find F values substantially larger than 1.0 most of the time; here they should expect F values closer to 11.9 than to 1.0. In other words, if the true effects of treatments is large, then they should expect to find large F values most of the time.

---

[1]Equations 4 and 5 are based on simple linear models, in which there is only one effect being tested, and the variance in scores is assumed to be due to either the effects of treatments or to error (e.g., this is the model that underlies the t test or the one-way analysis of variance). In more complex linear models, v2 does not necessarily refer to the degrees of freedom associated with variability in scores of individuals who receive the same treatment (within-cell variability in the one-way ANOVA model), and a more general form of Equation 5 ($\lambda_{est} = [(N - k) * (PV/1 - PV))]$, where N represents the number of observations and k represents the total number of terms in the linear model) is needed. When N is large, Equation 5 yields very similar results to those of the more general form shown earlier.

The larger the effect, the larger the noncentrality parameter, and the larger the expected value of F. The larger the F, the more likely researchers are to reject H_0. Therefore—all other things being equal—the more noncentrality (i.e., the larger the effect), the higher the power.

Using the Noncentral F Distribution to Assess Power

Chapter 1 laid out the three steps in conducting a statistical power analysis (i.e., determine critical value for significance, estimate effect size, estimate proportion of test statistics likely to exceed critical value). If these steps are applied here, it follows that power analysis involves the following:

1. Deciding what value of F is needed to reject H_0. As pointed out later in this chapter, this depends in part on the specific hypothesis being tested.
2. Estimating the effect size and the degree of noncentrality. Estimates of PV allow researchers to estimate the noncentrality parameter of the F distribution.
3. Estimating the proportion of the noncentral F distribution (using the λ value from step 2) that lies above the critical F from step 1.

The chapters that follow present a simple method of conducting power analyses for a wide range of hypotheses that relies on the noncentral F distribution. Appendix A discusses approaches to both approximating and calculating the noncentral F distribution. Appendix B presents a table of F values obtained by estimating the noncentral F distribution over a range of v1, v2, and effect size values.[2] This table saves researchers the difficulty of estimating noncentral F values, and more important, of directly computing power estimates for each statistical test performed. This table can be used to test both traditional and minimum-effect null hypotheses, as well as to estimate the statistical power of tests of both types of hypotheses.

A Note on Approximations

The methods described in this chapter are simple and general, but they are not always precise to the last decimal place. There are many statistical procedures that fall under the general linear model um-

---

[2]As noted in Appendix A, all tables presented in this book are based on the cumulative distribution function for the noncentral F. The precision of these tables has been assessed extensively, and the values presented in these tables allow for the reconstruction with considerable accuracy the power tables presented by J. Cohen (1988) and in other standard works.

brella, and some specific applications of this model may present unique complications, or distributional complexities. However, the methods developed here provide acceptably accurate approximations for the entire range of statistical tests covered under this general model. Approximations are particularly appropriate for statistical power analysis because virtually all applications of this technique are themselves approximations, because the population effect size is never known for sure. That is, real-world applications of power analysis rarely depend on precise estimates, but rather depend on obtaining reasonable estimates to help inform decisions. Thus, a good approximation is quite acceptable.

For example, power analysis might be used to guide the selection of sample sizes or significance criteria in a study. Power analysis typically functions as a decision aid rather than as a precise forecasting technique, and it is rare that different decisions will be reached when exact versus approximate power values are known. That is, users of power analysis are likely to reach the same decisions if they know that power is about .80 in a particular study as they would reach if they knew that the power was precisely .815 for that study.

Statistical power analysis is an area where precision is not of sufficient value to justify the use of cumbersome methods in pursuit of the last decimal place. As a result, it is possible to use the general method developed here to approximate, with a high degree of precision, the more specific findings obtained when power analyses are tailored to specific analytic techniques (see J. Cohen, 1988, for discussions of power analysis for each of several types of statistical tests). The approach described here allows researchers to estimate statistical power for statistical tests in the general linear model by translating specific test statistics or effect size measures into their equivalent F values.

TRANSLATING COMMON STATISTICS AND EFFECT SIZE MEASURES INTO F

The model developed here is expressed in terms of the F statistic, which is commonly reported in analysis of variance and multiple regression. However, many studies may report their results in terms of something other than an F value. It is useful, therefore, to have at hand formulas for translating common statistics and effect size measures (e.g., d) into their F equivalents. Table 2.1 presents a set of formulas for doing just that.

For example, a study compared the effectiveness of two smoking cessation programs in a sample of 120 adults, who are randomly assigned to treatments, and used the t test to compare scores in these two groups. The reported t value of 2.48 would be equivalent to an F value of 6.15, with 1 and 118 degrees of freedom. A study ($N = 112$) that reported a multiple correlation of .45 between a set of four vocational interest tests and occupational choice measure would yield an F value of 9.06, with 3 and 107 degrees of freedom.

Hierarchical regression is used to determine the incremental contribution of k new predictor variables over and above the set of predictor variables already in an equation. For example, in a study with $N = 250$, two spatial ability tests were used to predict performance as an aircraft pilot; scores on these tests explained 14% of the variability in pilots' performance (i.e., $R^2 = .14$). Four tests measuring other cognitive abilities were added to the predictor battery, and this set of six tests explained 29% of the variance in performance (i.e., $R^2 = .29$). The F statistic that corresponds to this increase in R^2 is $F(4, 243) = 12.83$.

As Table 2.1 shows, χ^2 values can be translated in F equivalents. For example, if researchers found a χ^2 value of 24.56 with 6 degrees of freedom, the equivalent F value is 4.10, with v1 = 6 and v2 being infinite. Because the F table asymptotes as v2 grow larger, v2 = 10,000 (which is included on the F Table listed in Appendix B) represents an excellent approximation to infinite degrees of freedom for the error term.

Table 2.1 also includes the effect size measure d. This statistic is not commonly used in hypothesis testing per se, but it is widely used in describing the strength of effects, particularly when the scores of those receiving the treatment are compared to scores in a control group. Suppose that previous research suggests that the effect size d should be about .25. A study in which 102 subjects were randomly assigned to one of two treatments would be expected to yield an F value of 1.56, with 1 and 100 degrees of freedom. If d was .50, an F value of 6.25 would be expected. If researchers used a repeated measures design (e.g., one in which scores of 101 subjects on a pretest and a posttest were compared, with a correlation of .60 between these scores), F would be 9.78.

Note that sample size was included in the previous examples. The reason for this is that the value and the interpretation of the F statistic depends in part on the size of the sample (in particular, on the degrees of freedom for the error term, or v2). In the preceding paragraph, a d value of .25 in a sample of 102 would yield $F(1,100) = 1.56$. In a

TABLE 2.1

Translating Common Statistics into F-equivalent Values

Statistic	F-equivalent	Degrees of Freedom	
		v1	v2
t test for difference between means	$F(1, v2) = t^2$	-	N - 2
Correlation coefficient	$F(1, v2) = \dfrac{r^2 v2}{(1 - r^2)}$	-	N - 2
Multiple R^2	$F(v1, v2) = \dfrac{R^2 v2}{(1 - R^2)v1}$	p	N - p - 1
Hierarchical regression	$F(v1, v2) = \dfrac{(R^2{}_F - R^2{}_R)v2}{(1 - R^2{}_F)v1}$	k	N - p - 1
Chi-squared (χ^2)	$F(v1, v2) = \chi^2 / v1$	v1	∞
difference	$F(1, v2) = \dfrac{d^2 v2}{4}$	-	N - 2

| d (repeated measures) | $F(1, v2) = \dfrac{d^2 v2}{4\sqrt{1 - r_{ab}}}$ | $N - 2$ |

Note: p = number of X variables in multiple regression equation. R^2_F and R^2_R represent the full and restricted model R^2 values, respectively, where the k represents the difference in the number of X variables in the two models. A χ^2 variable with df = v1 is distributed as F with df of v1 and ¥. When d is used to describe the difference between two measures obtained from the same sample, r_{ab} refers to the the correlation between the two measures being compared.

sample of 227, the same d would translate into $F\,(1{,}225) = 3.52$. This reflects the fact that the same difference between means is easier to statistically detect when the sample (and therefore v2) is large than when the sample is small. Small samples produce unstable and unreliable results, and in a small sample it can be hard to distinguish between true treatment effects and simple sampling error.

Finally, a note concerning terminology. In the previous section, and in several sections that follow, the term F equivalent is used. This term is used to be explicit in recognizing that even when the results of a statistical test in the general linear model are reported in terms of some statistic other than F (e.g., r^{xy}, t, d), it is nevertheless very often possible to estimate the F value that is equivalent in meaning.

Transforming From F to PV

Table 2.1 shows how to transform commonly used statistics and effect size estimates into their equivalent F values. It is also useful to transform from F values to an equivalent effect size measure. For example, suppose researchers used analysis of variance to analyze their data, reported a significant F value, but did not provide information about the strength of the effect. Equations 6 and 7 allow them to obtain an estimate of the proportion of variance in the dependent variable explained by the linear model (i.e., PV), given the value of F:

$$f^2 = (v1 * F) / v2 \tag{6}$$

$$PV = f^2 / (1 + f^2) \tag{7}$$

The f^2 in Equations 6 and 7 is the squared value of the effect size estimator f discussed in J. Cohen (1988). For example, if a study reports $F\,(3, 60) = 2.80$, this implies that treatments account for about

12% of the variance in the dependent variable. As is pointed out later in this chapter, formulas for transforming effect size estimates to their F equivalents, or F values to equivalent effect size estimates, are extremely useful in conducting power analyses.

Equations 6 and 7 can be combined into a single, simple formula for estimating PV on the basis of F and degrees of freedom:

$$PV = \frac{v1\,F}{v1F + v2} \tag{8}$$

Nonparametric and Robust Statistics

The decision to anchor the discussion of statistical power analysis to the F distribution is driven primarily by the ubiquitousness of statistical tests based on that distribution. The F statistic can be used to test virtually any hypothesis that falls under the broad umbrella of the general linear model, but there are some important statistics that do not fall under this umbrella, and are not handled by the model developed and discussed here.

For example, a number of *robust*, or *trimmed*, statistics have been developed in which outliers are removed from observed distributions prior to estimating standard errors and test statistics (Wilcox, 1992; Yuen, 1974). Trimming outliers can sometimes substantially reduce the effects of sampling error, and trimmed statistics can have more power than their normal-theory equivalents (Wilcox, 1992). The power tables developed in this book are not fully appropriate for trimmed statistics, and can substantially underestimate the power of these statistics when applied in small samples.

A second family of statistics not easily accommodated using the model developed here are referred to as *nonparametric*. In general, nonparametric statistics do not make a priori assumptions about distributional forms, and tend to use little information about the observed distribution of data in constructing statistical tests. The conventional wisdom has long been that nonparametric tests have less power than their parametric equivalents (Siegel, 1956), but this is not always the case. Nonparametric tests can have more power than their parametric equivalents under a variety of circumstances, especially when conducting tests using distributions with heavy tails (Zimmerman & Zumbo, 1993). The methods developed here provide only gross approximations when used to assess the power of robust or nonparametric equivalents of standard statistical tests.

ALTERNATIVES TO THE TRADITIONAL
NULL HYPOTHESIS

The traditional null hypothesis is that treatments, interventions, and so on have no effect. There are two advantages to testing this hypothesis: It is easy (i.e., tests of this hypothesis are the standard fare for statistics courses, textbooks, data analysis packages, etc.) and if the hypothesis that treatments have no effect is rejected, what is left is the alternative that they have some effect. However, as noted earlier, this approach to statistical analysis has increasingly come under attack (J. Cohen, 1994; Meehl, 1978; Morrison & Henkel, 1970; Murphy, 1990; Schmidt, 1992, 1996. For discussions of the advantages of this approach, see Chow, 1988; Cortina & Dunlap, 1997; Hagen, 1997). The most general criticism of this approach is that nobody actually believes the null hypothesis. By definition, the traditional null hypothesis is usually treated as false, which means that tests of this hypothesis are not necessarily meaningful (Murphy, 1990).

Second, the outcomes of tests of the traditional null hypothesis are routinely misinterpreted. As is noted later, the outcomes of standard statistical tests probably say more about the power of the study than about the phenomenon being studied.

Why Is the Traditional Null Hypothesis Always Wrong?

The reason the traditional null hypothesis is formally wrong is that it is a *point hypothesis*. That is, the hypothesis being tested is that the effect of treatments is exactly nil, even to the millionth decimal place or beyond. A treatment that has an obviously negligible effect will nevertheless lead to the rejection of the traditional null, as long as a large enough sample can be assembled.

The traditional null hypothesis represents a convenient abstraction, similar to the mythical "friction-less plane" encountered by freshmen in solving physics problems. There are many real-world phenomena that seem to mirror the traditional null hypothesis, the most obvious being flipping a coin (see Fick, 1995, for examples that show how the traditional null could be correct). However, even in studies that involved repeated flips of a fair coin, the traditional null is, by definition, wrong. The traditional null hypothesis is that there is no difference whatsoever in the probability of getting a head or a tail. In fact, it is impossible to mill a coin that is so precisely balanced that this will be true. Even if it is balanced to the billionth of the ounce, the traditional null is still wrong—imbalance at the ten-billionth of the ounce will lead to the rejection of traditional null if the study is sufficiently sensitive.

The traditional null hypothesis is virtually always wrong because it is infinitely precise, and none of the real-world phenomena it is designed to test can possibly be measured with that level of precision. The same can be said for any point hypothesis (e.g., the hypothesis that the difference between two methods of reading instruction is exactly six points). The argument against the traditional null is not only a philosophical one; there are also abundant data to suggest that treatments in the social and behavioral sciences virtually always have at least some effect (Lipsey & Wilson, 1993; Murphy & Myors, 1997). In fact, it may not be possible to devise a real treatment that has no effect whatsoever; the hypothesis that treatments have no effect is so unlikely to be true that tests of this hypothesis are sometimes meaningless (Murphy, 1990).

The fact that the traditional null hypothesis is virtually always wrong has important implications for thinking about Type I and Type II errors. If the null hypothesis is wrong, it is impossible to make a Type I error (i.e., to reject H_0 when it is true), and the only error that should cause concern is a Type II error (i.e., failing to reject H_0 when you should). If researchers accept the position that the traditional null hypothesis is virtually never true, then it follows that they should be much more concerned with statistical power than with the control of Type I errors.

Significance Tests Are Routinely Misinterpreted

Showing that a result is significant at the .05 level does not necessarily imply that it is important or is especially likely to be replicated in a future study (J. Cohen, 1994). It merely shows that the particular findings being tested would probably not have been found if the true effect of treatments was zero. Unfortunately, researchers routinely misinterpret the results of these tests (J. Cohen, 1994; Cowles, 1989; Greenwald, 1993). This is entirely understandable; most dictionary definitions of "significant" include synonyms such as "important" or "weighty." However, these tests do not directly assess the size or importance of treatment effects.

Tests of the traditional null hypothesis are more likely to tell researchers about the sensitivity of their study than about the phenomenon being studied. With large samples, statistical tests of the traditional null hypothesis become so sensitive that they can detect any difference between a sample result and the specific value that characterized the null hypothesis, even if this difference is negligibly small. With small samples, on the other hand, it is difficult to establish that anything has a statistically significant effect. The best way to get an appreciation of the limitations of traditional null hypothesis tests is to scan the tables in any power analysis book (J. Cohen, 1988). What researchers will find is that, regardless of the true strength of the effect, the likelihood of rejecting the traditional null hypothesis is very small when samples are small, and is virtually certain when samples are large. Clearly, there is a need for approaches to significance testing that tell them more about the phenomenon being studied than about the size of their samples. Alternatives to traditional null hypothesis tests are described later.

MINIMUM-EFFECT TESTS AS ALTERNATIVES TO TRADITIONAL NULL HYPOTHESIS TESTS

Rather than abandoning null hypothesis testing altogether, it is better to reform the process. The problem with most null hypotheses is that the specific hypothesis being tested (i.e., that treatments have no effect whatsoever) is neither credible nor informative (Murphy, 1990); J. Cohen (1994) dismissed this approach as testing the "nil hypothesis." As noted earlier, there are several alternatives to testing the nil hypothesis, and all of these are a marked improvement over the standard procedure of testing the hypothesis that the effects of treatments is precisely zero. Serlin and Lapsley (1993) showed how researchers can test the hypothesis that the effect of treatments falls within or outside of some range of values that is "good enough" to establish that one treatment is meaningfully better than the other. Rouanet (1996) showed how Bayesian methods can be used to assert the importance or negligibility of treatment effects. Both of these methods allow researchers to directly test credible and meaningful hypotheses.

There is much to be learned by conducting tests of a substantive null hypothesis, such as the hypothesis that effects of treatments are negligibly small (e.g., they account for 1% or less of the variance in outcomes). In contrast to tests of the traditional null, tests of this sort are far from trivial (i.e., it is not known in advance whether H_0 is wrong), and they involve questions that are of real substantive interest. First, because they include some range of values rather than a single exact point under the *null umbrella*, the results of these tests are not a foregone conclusion. Although it might be impossible to devise a treatment, intervention, and so on, that had no effect whatsoever, there are any number of treatments whose effects fall somewhere between zero and whatever point is chosen as a negligible effect. The possibility that the treatments will have a negligibly small effect is both real and meaningful (whereas the possibility that they will have no effect whatsoever is not), and something important can be learned about the treatments by testing this hypothesis.

It was previously noted that when testing the traditional null hypothesis, researchers can guarantee the outcome if the sample is sufficiently large. That is, with a sufficiently sensitive study, the statistical power of tests of the traditional null hypothesis can reach 1.00. The same is not true when testing the hypothesis that the effect of treatment exceeds some negligible minimum. Because there is a real possibility that the effect of treatments will not exceed that minimum, the upper bound of the power of these alternative tests will generally be lower than 1.00. No matter how good the study, researchers will never be certain in advance of the result of such a test. This may be regarded as a good thing. One major criticism of tests of the traditional null is that they are literally pointless (Murphy, 1990). Because it is known in advance that the traditional H_0 is wrong, nothing new is really learned about H_0, regardless of the outcome of the significance test. Minimum-effect tests, on the other hand, can be informative, particularly if they have acceptable levels of statistical power. If there is a great deal of power and there is still a failure to reject the hypothesis that a treatment effect is at best negligible, this would be regarded as strong evidence that the effect is negligible.

Testing the Hypothesis that Treatment Effects Are Negligible

The best way to describe the process of testing a minimum-effect hypothesis is to compare it to the process used in testing the traditional null. The significance of the F statistic is usually assessed by comparing the value of the F obtained in a study to the value listed in an F table. The tabled values correspond to specific percentiles in the central F distribution. For example, if $v1 = 2$ and $v2 = 100$, the tabled values of F are 3.09 and 4.82, for $\alpha = .05$ and $\alpha = .01$, respectively. In other words, if the null hypothesis is true and there are 2 and 100 degrees of freedom, it should be expected to find F values of 3.09 or lower 95% of the time, and values of 4.82 or lower 99% of the time. If the F is larger than these values, then the null hypothesis will be rejected.

Tests of minimum-effect hypotheses proceed in exactly the same way, only using a different set of tabled F values (Murphy & Myors, 1997). The F tables found in the back of most statistics texts are based on the central F distribution, or the distribution of the F statistic that would be expected if the traditional null hypothesis were true. Tests of minimum-effect hypotheses are based on the noncentral F distribution. For example, suppose it is decided that treatments that account for 1% or less of the variance in outcomes have a "negligible" effect. It is then possible to estimate a noncentrality parameter (based on $PV = .01$), and to estimate the corresponding noncentral F distribution for testing the hypothesis that treatment effects are at best negligible. If $PV = .01$, $v1 = 2$, and $v2 = 100$, then 95% of the values in this noncentral F distribution will fall at or below 4.49; and 99% of the values in this distribution will fall at or below 6.76 (as is noted later, F values for testing minimum-effect hypotheses are listed in Appendix B). In other words, if the observed F in the study was greater than 4.49, researchers could be confident ($\alpha = .05$) in rejecting the hypothesis that treatments accounted for 1% or less of the variance. Later in this chapter, standards that might be used in designating effects as negligible are discussed.

Notice that minimum-effect hypotheses involve specifying a whole range of values as negligible. In the previous example, effects that account for 1% or less of the variance in the population were designated as negligible effects, and if the hypothesis that the effects are negligibly small can be rejected, what is left is the alternative hypothesis that they are not negligibly small (i.e., that treatment effects are large enough to care about). But how can a single critical F value allow researchers to test for a whole range of null possibilities? Remember, one characteristic of the F statistic is that it ranges from zero to infinity, with larger F values indicating larger effects. Therefore, if it is possible to be 95% confident that the observed F is larger than the F that would have been obtained if treatments accounted for 1% of the variance, it is also possible to be at least 95% confident that the observed F would be larger than that which would have been obtained for any PV value between .00 and .01. If the observed F is larger than the F values expected 95% of the time when $PV = .01$, then it must also be larger than 95% of the values expected for any smaller PV value.

An Example

Suppose 125 subjects are randomly assigned to one of five treatments. It is found that $F(4, 120) = 2.50$, and that in this sample, treatments account for 7.6% of the variance in the dependent variable. The F is large enough to allow the rejection of the traditional null hypothesis ($\alpha = .05$), but there is concern that the true effect of treatments might be negligibly small. Suppose also that in this context, treatments that account for less than 1% of the variance in the population have effects that are considered to be "negligible." To test the hypothesis that the effects observed here came from a population in which the true effect of treatments is negligibly small, consult the noncentral F distribution with $v1 = 4$, $v2 = 120$, and $\lambda = 1.21$ (i.e., $\lambda_{est} = [120 * .01]/[1 - .01]$). This will show that 95% of the values in this distribution are 3.13 or lower. The obtained F of 2.50, which is smaller than this critical value, means that this null hypothesis cannot be rejected. That is, although the hypothesis that treatments have no effect whatsoever (i.e., the traditional null) can be rejected, the hypothesis that the effects of treatments are negligibly small (i.e., a minimum-effect hypothesis) cannot be rejected. In other words, it is possible that treatments that have essentially no effect in the population (i.e., that explain less than 1% of the variance in the dependent variable) might nevertheless have what appears to be a reasonably large effect in a sample.

Defining a Minimum Effect

The main advantage of the traditional null hypothesis is that it is simple and objective. If researchers reject the hypothesis that treatments have no effect, they are left with the alternative that they have some effect. On the other hand, testing minimum-effect hypotheses requires a value judgment, and requires that some consensus be reached in a particular field of inquiry. For example, the definition of a negligible effect might reasonably vary across areas, and there may be no set convention for defining which effects are so small that they can be effectively ignored and which cannot. However, it is possible to offer some broad principles for determining when effects are likely to be judged negligible.

First, the importance of an effect might depend substantially on the particular dependent variables involved. For example, in medical research, it is common for relatively small effects (in terms of the percentage of variance explained) to be viewed as meaningful and important (Rosenthal, 1993). One reason is that the dependent variables in these studies often include quality of life, and even survival. A small percentage of variance might translate into many lives saved.

Second, decisions about what effects should be labeled as negligible might depend on the relative likelihood and relative seriousness of Type I versus Type II errors in a particular area. As is noted in a section to come, the power of statistical tests in the general linear model decreases as the definition of a negligible effect expands. In any particular study, power is higher for testing the traditional null hypothesis that treatments have no effect than for testing the hypothesis that they account for 1% or less of the variance in outcomes, and higher for tests of the hypothesis that treatments account for 1% or less of the variance than for the hypothesis that treatments account for 5% or less of the variance in outcomes. If Type II errors are seen as particularly serious in a particular area of research, then it might make sense to choose a very low figure as the definition of a negligible effect.

On the other hand, there are many areas of inquiry in which numerous well-validated treatments are already available (See Lipsey & Wilson, 1993, for a review of numerous metanalyses of treatment effects), and in these areas, it might make sense to "set a higher bar" by testing a more demanding hypothesis. For example, in the area of cognitive ability testing (where the criterion is some measure of performance on the job or in the classroom), it is common to find that tests account for 20–25% of the variance in the criterion (J. E. Hunter & R. F. Hunter, 1984; J. E. Hunter & Hirsch, 1987). Tests of the traditional null hypothesis (i.e., that tests have no relation whatsoever to these criteria) are relatively easy to reject; if $\rho_2 = .25$, a study with $N = 28$ will have power of .80 for rejecting the traditional null hypothesis (J. Cohen, 1988). Similarly, the hypothesis that tests account for 1% or less of the variance in these criteria is easy to reject; if $\rho_2 = .25$, a study with $N = 31$ will have power of .80 for rejecting this minimum-effect hypothesis (Murphy & Myors, 1997). In this context, it might make sense to define a negligible relation as one in which tests accounted for 10% or less of the variance in these criteria.

Utility analysis has been used to help determine whether particular treatments have effects that are large enough to warrant attention (Landy, Farr, & Jacobs, 1982; Schmidt, J. E. Hunter, McKenzie, & Muldrow, 1979; Schmidt, Mack, & J. E. Hunter, 1984). Utility equations suggest another important parameter that is likely to affect the decision of what represents a negligible versus a meaningful effect (i.e., the standard deviation of the dependent variable, or SD_y). When there is substantial and meaningful variance in the outcome variable of interest, a treatment that accounts for a relatively small percentage of variance might nevertheless lead to practical benefits that far exceed the costs of the treatment.

For example, suppose a training program costs $1,000 per person to administer, and that it is proposed as a method of improving performance in a setting where the current SD_y (i.e., the standard deviation of performance) is $10,000. If the effects of training account for less than 1% of the variation in job performance, it might be concluded that the projected cost of training will exceed the projected benefit (based on the equation $\Delta U = r_{xy} * SD_y - C$, where ΔU is the projected overall benefit, r_{xy} is the relation between the training and the criterion—in this case, $PV = .01$ translates into $r_{xy} = .10$ and C represents the cost), which suggests that $PV = .01$ represents a sensible definition of the minimum effect needed to label training effects as "nontrivial."

Many of the examples presented in this book use conventions similar to those described in J. Cohen (1988), describing treatments that have less than 1% of the variance as having small effects, and those that account for less than 5% of the variance in outcomes as having small to medium effects (these conventions are discussed in detail later in this chapter). Many of the tables presented are arranged around these particular conventions. However, it is critical to note that the decision of what represents a negligible effect is one that is likely to vary across research areas, and there will be many cases in which these particular conventions do not apply. Appendix A presents the information needed to determine critical F values for minimum-effect tests that employ some other operational definition of "negligible", and researchers are urged to carefully consider their reasons for choosing any particular value as a definition of the minimum effect of interest.

Power of Minimum-Effect Tests

As this example suggests, researchers should expect less power when testing the hypothesis that the effect in the study exceeds some minimum value than when testing the hypothesis that it is exactly zero. The traditional hypothesis that treatments have no effect whatsoever is, by definition, wrong (Murphy, 1990), and is therefore relatively easy to reject. If the sample is large enough, the hypothesis that treatments have no effect will always be rejected, even if the true effect of treatments is extremely negligible. Tests of the hypothesis that treatment effects exceed whatever lower bound is used to define negligible are more demanding than tests of the traditional null, in part because there is always a chance that the effects are negligible. Therefore, there is no guarantee that researchers will reject the hypothesis, no matter how sensitive the study. However, as is noted in several other chapters, the lower power of substantive tests is easily offset by the fact that these tests reveal something meaningful, regardless how large the sample size or how sensitive the study.

ANALYTIC AND TABULAR METHODS
OF POWER ANALYSIS

There are several methods available to carry out statistical power analyses. First, it is possible to compute either the approximate or exact level of power in any particular case. Analytic methods of power analysis are discussed later. Second, it is possible to develop tables or graphs that provide good approximations of the statistical power of studies under a wide range of conditions. The preference here is to work with tables, because in part the type of graphs needed to plot a variable (i.e., power) as a function of three other variables (i.e., N, α, and ES) seem complicated and difficult to use. As is shown later, it is possible to generate tables that neatly integrate information about traditional and minimum-effect hypothesis tests with information about statistical power.

Analytic Methods

The previous section demonstrated the analytic approach to power analysis using either an approximation to or a relatively exact calculation of the noncentral F distribution. It is possible to apply this approach to calculate the power of any test that can be framed in terms of the familiar F statistic. All that is needed is a calculator and a fairly detailed table of the widely used central F distribution (a table that only gives critical values at the .05 and .01 levels will not always have the information needed to calculate power). Appendix A discusses several methods of estimating values in the noncentral F distribution.

Although this analytic method is both precise and flexible, it is also relatively cumbersome and time consuming. That is, the direct computation of statistical power involves: determining some standard for statistical or practical significance (e.g., setting a minimum value for a negligible effect), estimating the noncentral F distribution that applies, and determining the proportion of that distribution that lies above the standard. Even with a relatively powerful computer, the processes can be time consuming, and may be daunting to many consumers of power analysis. A more user-friendly approach is to develop tables that contain the essential information needed to estimate statistical power.

Power Tables

A number of excellent books present extensive tables describing the statistical power of numerous tests; J. Cohen (1988) is the most complete source currently available. The approach espoused here is simpler (although it provides a bit less information), but considerably more compact. All of the information needed to do most significance tests and power analyses for statistical tests in the general linear model is presented in Appendix B, which contains what is called the "One-Stop F Table." This is called a "one stop" table because each cell contains the information needed for: conducting traditional significance tests, conducting power analyses at various key levels of power, testing the hypothesis that the effect in a study exceeds various criteria used to define negligibly small or small to moderate effects, and estimating power for these "minimum-effect" tests.

USING THE ONE-STOP F TABLE

Each cell in the One-Stop F Table contains 12 pieces of information. The first 4 values in each cell are used for testing significance and estimating power for traditional null hypothesis tests. The next 8 values in each cell are used for testing significance and estimating power when testing the hypothesis that treatment effects are negligible, using two different operational definitions of a negligible effect (i.e., treatments account for 1% or less of the variance, or that they account for 5% or less of the variance).

To illustrate the use of this table, consider another study. Fifty-four subjects are randomly assigned to one of four treatments. The treatment being studied is one believed to have at least a moderate effect (e.g., treatments are expected to account for about 15% of the variance). It is found that F (3, 50) = 3.50, and that treatments account for 17.3% of the variance in your sample.

Traditional Null Hypothesis Tests

The first four values in each cell of the One-Stop F Table are used for hypothesis testing and power analysis when testing the traditional null hypothesis (i.e., that treatments have no effect). The first value in each cell of this table represents the critical F for the traditional null hypothesis significance test, with an alpha level of .05. In the previous example, v1 = 3 and v2 = 50, which yields a critical F of 2.79. If the observed F value in the study exceeds 2.79 (as was the case here), H_0 would be rejected. The second value in each cell is the critical F for the traditional null hypothesis test at the .01 level of significance (F needs to be greater than or equal to 4.20 to reject the traditional null hypothesis at the .01 level). The F of 3.50 found in the study would allow the traditional null to be rejected with $\alpha = .05$, but not with $\alpha = .01$.

The next two values in each cell are F equivalents of the effect size values needed to obtain particular levels of power (given an α level of 0.05 and the specified v1 and v2). The values in the table are 1.99 and 3.88, respectively, for power levels of .50 and .80, respectively. If equations 6 and 7 are used to transform these values into equivalent PV values, the values of .11 and .19, respectively are found. That is, power would be .50 for rejecting the traditional null if treatments accounted for about 11% of the variance in the population, and power would be .80 if treatments accounted for about 18% of the variance. In fact, it should be expected that the population effect is somewhere between these two figures (i.e., treatments account for about 15% of the variance), which implies that the power of the study is in the range .50 to .80. As is shown later in this chapter, it is easy to estimate where in this range the power of the study actually falls (in this example, power is approximately .65).

Testing Minimum-Effect Hypotheses ($PV = .01$)

Rather than testing the hypothesis that treatments have no effect whatsoever, researchers might want to test the hypothesis that treatment effects are so small that they account for less than 1% of the variance in outcomes. If this PV value represents a sensible definition of a negligible effect in a particular area of research, and this hypothesis is tested and rejected, they can be confident that effects are not negligibly small.

The 5th and 6th values in each cell of the One-Stop F Table are the critical F values needed to be obtained in order to achieve significance (at the .05 and .01 levels, respectively) when testing the hypothesis that treatments account for 1% or less of the variance in outcomes. With v1 = 3 and v2 = 50, F needs to be 3.24 to reject (with $\alpha = .05$) the hypothesis that the effect being studied was negligibly small (defined as accounting for 1% or less of the variance in outcomes). The obtained F was 3.50, meaning that both the traditional null hypothesis and the hypothesis that the effect is negligibly small can be rejected. However, if a .01 alpha level is used, the obtained F will be smaller than the tabled F value of 4.85. With an alpha level of .01, researchers will not be able to reject either the traditional null or the hypothesis that the observed effect is negligibly small.

The 7th and 8th values in each cell are F equivalents of the effect size values needed to obtain particular levels of power (given an α level of .05 and the specified v1 and v2) for testing this substantive hypothesis. The values in the table are 2.46 and 4.48 for power levels of .50 and .80, respectively. This translates into PV values of .13 and .21, respectively. That is, if treatments accounted for 13% of the variance in the population, a study with v1 = 3, v2 = 50, and α = .05 would have power of about .50. If treatments account for 21% of the variance in the population, power would be approximately .80.

In this study, it was expected that treatments would account for about 15% of the variance. This analysis suggests that power for testing the hypothesis that the population effect is negligibly small is somewhere between .50 and .80 (in this example, power is approximately .57). Chapter 3 shows how to determine where in this range the power of this study lies.

Testing Minimum-Effect Hypotheses (PV = .05)

There are many treatments that routinely demonstrate moderate to large effects. For example, well-developed cognitive ability tests allow researchers to predict performance in school and in many jobs with a relatively high degree of success (correlations in the .30 to .50 range are common). Rather than testing the hypothesis that tests have no relation whatsoever with these criteria (i.e., the traditional null), or even that treatments account for 1% or less of the variance in outcomes, it might make sense to test a more challenging hypothesis (i.e., that the effect of this particular treatment is at least small to moderate in size). For reasons explained in the next section, there are many contexts in which it is useful to test the hypothesis that treatments explain 5% or less of the variance in the population. If the hypothesis that effects explain 5% or less of the variance in outcomes is tested and rejected, what is left is the alternative that treatments explain more than 5% of the variance. In most contexts, effects this large are likely to be treated as meaningful, even if smaller effects (e.g., those accounting for 1% of the variance) are not treated as such.

The 9th and 10th values in each cell of the One-Stop F Table are the critical F values needed in order to achieve significance (at the .05 and .01 levels, respectively) when testing the hypothesis that treatments account for 5% or less of the variance in outcomes. With v1 = 3 and v2 = 50, you would need an F of 4.84 would be needed to reject (with α = .05) the hypothesis that the effect being studied was no greater than small to moderate in size. The obtained F was 3.50, meaning that this hypothesis cannot be rejected (if $\alpha = .01$, researchers would need $F = 6.98$ to reject this null). In other words, the findings of the study are not sufficiently strong to reject the possibility that the real population effect is smaller than what has been defined as the small to moderate range (i.e., $PV = .05$ or lower).

The 11th and 12th values in each cell are F equivalents of the effect size values needed to obtain particular levels of power (given an α level of 0.05 and the specified v1 and v2) for tests of this minimum-effect hypothesis. The values in the table are 4.08 and 6.55 for power levels of .50 and .80, respectively. This translates into PV values of .24 and .39, respectively. It was expected that treatments would account for about 15% of the variance. This analysis suggests that the power for testing the hypothesis that this population effect is small to moderate (i.e., that it accounts for more than 5% of the variance in outcomes) is well below .50. In other words, this particular study does not have sufficient power for a credible test of this hypothesis. With this combination of ES, sample size, and significance criteria, a significance test is almost like the flip of a coin.

To review what this table reveals about a study, in which it was found that $F(3, 50) = 3.50$, and that treatments account for 17% of the variance in the sample, both the traditional null and the hypothesis that treatment effects are negligibly small with an alpha of .05 can be rejected; with alpha of .01 neither hypothesis can be rejected. With an alpha level of .05, the table suggests that the power of tests of the traditional null hypothesis is between .50 and .80 (the actual power level is about .65). This study also has power slightly greater than .50 for testing the hypothesis that treatment effects are negligible (i.e., that the population PV is .01 or less). However, the hypothesis that treatments explain 5% or less of the variance in the population cannot be rejected.

Note that the One-Stop F Table does not contain a set of rows corresponding to relatively large effects (i.e., effects accounting for more than 5% of the variance in outcomes). As was noted in chapter 1, when the effect of treatments is known or thought to be large, there is often no point to conducting the research. Large effects are usually so obvious that a study confirming their existence is unlikely to make much of a contribution. More to the point, when the effects under consideration are large, statistical power is unlikely to be a problem unless samples are extremely small. When samples are this small, researchers have problems that are much more severe than statistical power (e.g., lack of generalizability), and power analyses for large effects seem very limited in value.

Interpolating Between Tabled Values

Like all F tables, the One-Stop F Table is incomplete in that it does not table all possible values of v1 and v2. Fortunately, relatively good approximations to all of the values in this table can be obtained by linear interpolation. For example, the table includes v2 values of 50 and 60. Appropriate F values for v2 = 55 would lie about halfway between the values for v2 = 50 and v2 = 60. Thus, the approximate F needed to reject the traditional null hypothesis (α = .05) with v1 = 2, v2 = 55 would be 3.165 (i.e., halfway between 3.15 and 3.18). Similarly, if v2 = 48, the appropriate F values could be estimated by computing the value that F that was 80% of the distance between the tabled F for v2 = 40 and the tabled F for v2 = 50. In general, the value of the interpolated F can be obtained using the following formula:

$$F_{Interpolated} = F_{Below} + \left(\left(\frac{v2_{int} - v2_{below}}{v2_{above} - v2_{below}} \right) \left(F_{Above} - F_{Below} \right) \right) \qquad [9]$$

where:

F_{Below} = Tabled F below the value to be calculated

F_{Above} = Tabled F above the value to be calculated

$v2_{below}$ = v2 for tabled F below the value to be calculated

$v2_{above}$ = v2 for tabled F above the value to be calculated

$v2_{int}$ = v2 for F value to be calculated

It is important to keep in mind that linear interpolation will yield approximate values only. For the purposes of statistical power analyses, these interpolations will virtually always be sufficiently accurate to help researchers make sensible decisions about the design of studies, the choice of criteria for defining statistical significance, and so on.

A second application of linear interpolation is likely to be even more useful. The table includes F equivalents for the effect size values needed to obtain power levels of .50 and .80, respectively. In the example, where v1 = 3 and v2 = 50, F values of 1.99 and 3.88 are equivalent to the population PV values needed to obtain power levels of .50 or .80 in a study like this (i.e., you would achieve these levels of power if treatments truly accounted for 13% of the variance, yielding power of .50, or 21% of the variance, yielding power of .80). Here, treatments were expected to account for 15% of the variance. If this figure is translated into its F equivalent (using Equations 6 and 7 presented earlier), an F of 2.94 is obtained. A linear interpolation can be used to estimate the power of the study, using a formula that closely parallels the formula used to interpolate F values:

$$Power_{Interpolated} = .50 + \left[\left(\frac{F_{hypothesized} - F_{.50}}{F_{.80} - F_{.50}} \right) * .30 \right] \qquad [10]$$

where:

$F_{hypothesized}$ = F equivalent for hypothesized size of the effect

$F_{.50}$ = F equivalent of the PV needed to obtain power of .50 ($\alpha = .05$)

$F_{.80}$ = F equivalent of the PV needed to obtain power of .80 ($\alpha = .05$)

In the example, 54 subjects are assigned to one of four treatments ($v1 = 3$, $v2 = 50$), where treatments are expected to account for 15% of the variance, and where $\alpha = .05$. In this example, $F_{hypothesized} = 2.94$, $F_{.50} = 1.99$, and $F_{.80} = 3.88$. Using Equation 10, the estimate of power of this study for rejecting the traditional null hypothesis is .65. If the hypothesis tested was that treatments accounted for 1% or less of the variance, $F_{.50} = 2.46$, and $F_{.80} = 4.48$, and power is estimated to be .57.

Extrapolating outside of the tabled range of .50 to .80 is not recommended, and indeed estimating actual power levels when power is known to fall outside of these bounds does not make much difference. If power is above .80, it is unlikely that there will be different conclusions than if it was exactly .80, regardless of the outcome of a study. If power is below .50, there are more serious problems than the precise estimation of power.

EFFECT SIZE CONVENTIONS FOR DEFINING MINIMUM-EFFECT HYPOTHESES

Earlier in this chapter, it was noted that the best choice for PV values that defined negligible effects might depend on a number of factors, and that different values might make sense in different areas of research. However, some PV values seem more likely than others to be chosen in defining negligible effects. In particular, many researchers will choose either 1% of the variance (or less) or 5% of the variance (or less) as their operational definition of a negligible effect, which is why these particular values are built into the One-Stop F Table. These specific numbers are not cast in stone (any more than the commonly used p values of .05 and .01), but they do represent conventions that are somewhat widely used to describe effect sizes in the behavioral and social sciences.

J. Cohen's books and papers (1988) on statistical power analyses suggested a number of conventions for describing treatment effects as small, medium, or large. These conventions are based on surveys of the literature, and seem to be widely accepted, at least as approximations. Table 2.2 presents conventional values for describing large, medium, and small effects, expressing these effects in terms of a number of widely used statistics. For example, a small effect might be described as one that accounts for about 1% of the variance in outcomes, or one where the treatment mean is about 2/10 of a standard deviation higher in the treatment group than in the control group, or as one where the probability that a randomly selected member of the treatment group will have a higher score than a randomly selected member of the control group is about .56.

The values in Table 2.2 are approximations and nothing more. In fact, a few minutes with a calculator shows that they are not all exactly equivalent (e.g., if an r value of .30 is squared, what results is an estimate of $PV = .09$, not $PV = .10$). Although they are not exact or completely consistent, the values in Table 2.2 are nevertheless very useful. These conventions provide a starting point for statistical power analysis, and they provide a sensible basis for comparing the results in any one study with a more general set of conventions.

The One-Stop F Table includes F statistics for testing the substantive hypotheses that the effects of treatments are either at least small (i.e., 1% of the variance) or are at least small to moderate in size (i.e., 5% of the variance). It is possible to generate critical F values for any other set of conventions (Appendix A shows several methods of calculating the relevant noncentral F values for any PV value), but the utility of testing more and more stringent hypotheses (e.g., the hypothe-

TABLE 2.2
Some Conventions for Defining Effect Sizes

	PV	r	d	f^2	probability of a higher score in treatment group
Small effects	.01	.10	.20	.02	.56
Medium effects	.10	.30	.50	.15	.64
Large effects	.25	.50	.80	.35	.71

Note: From J. Cohen (1988) and Grissom (1994). Cohen's $f^2 = R^2/(1 - R^2) = \eta^2/(1 - \eta^2) = PV/(1 - PV)$, where $\eta^2 = SS_{treatments}/SS_{total}$.

sis that the effect of treatments is at least large) diminishes as the effect size of interest increases. When working with strong effects, statistical hypothesis tests (especially tests of null hypotheses) may become less and less informative. More to the point, most research in the social and behavioral sciences is likely to involve smaller rather than larger effects.

CONCLUSIONS

The statistics most widely used in the social and behavioral sciences are either interpreted in terms of, or easily translated into, the F statistic. The model for power analysis uses the noncentral F distribution to estimate the power of a wide range of statistics (cf. Patnaik, 1949). This noncentral F represents the distribution of outcomes that would be expected in any particular study (given an effect size, v1 and v2); the degree of noncentrality (λ) is a direct function of the effect size of interest. The statistical power of the study is simply the proportion of this noncentral F distribution that lies above whatever criterion is used to define statistical significance. This model of power analysis is not tied to tests of the traditional null hypothesis (i.e., that treatments had no effect whatsoever), but rather can be easily generalized to tests of substantively meaningful hypotheses (e.g., that the treatment effect exceeds some specific value).

Both analytic and tabular methods of statistical power analysis have been discussed. In particular, the One-Stop F Table, was introduced, which contains all of the information needed to test the traditional null hypothesis, estimate statistical power for testing this traditional null, test the substantive null hypothesis that the effect of treatments exceeds a sensible standard for defining negligible effects (e.g., that treatments account for no more than 1% of the variance in outcomes), and test the substantive null hypothesis that the effect of treatments exceeds a sensible standard for defining small to moderate effects (i.e., that treatments account for no more than 5% of the variance in outcomes). Finally, effect size estimates were discussed that are widely accepted as definitions of small, medium, and large effects in the social and behavioral sciences, and these were related to statistical power analysis.

3
Using Power Analyses

In chapter 1, it was noted that there are two general ways that power analysis might be used. First, power analysis is an extremely useful tool for planning research. Critical decisions, such as how many subjects are needed, whether multiple observations should be obtained from each subject, and even what criterion should be used to define statistical significance can be better made by taking into account the results of a power analysis. Decisions about whether or not to pursue a specific research question might even depend on considerations of statistical power. For example, if the research idea involves a small (but theoretically meaningful) interaction effect in a complex four-way ANOVA, power analysis might show that thousands of subjects would be needed to have any reasonable chance of detecting the effect. If the resources are not available to test for such an effect, it is certainly better to know this before the fact than to learn it after collecting data.

Second, power analysis is a useful diagnostic tool. Tests of the traditional null hypothesis often turn out to be little more than roundabout power analyses. If a study is conducted, and all of the correlations among variables, as well as all of the planned and unplanned comparisons between treatments turn out to be statistically significant, then this probably indicates a very large sample. If the sample is large enough, there will be tremendous power and any effect that is literally different from zero will also be statistically different from zero. On the other hand, if none of the researcher's well-conceived hypotheses are supported with significant results, a power analysis might be wise before asking what is wrong with their ideas. If the power is too low, they might never reject the null hypotheses, even in cases where it is clearly and obviously wrong.

This chapter discusses the major applications of power analysis. Chapter 1 noted that because statistical power is itself a function of three parameters, the number of observations (N), the criterion used to define statistical significance (α), and the effect size (ES), it is possible to solve for any one of four values (i.e., power, N, ES, or α), given the other three. The effect size parameter may be the most problematic, because it represents a real but unknown quantity (i.e, the real effect of the treatments). Before discussing practical applications of power analysis, it is useful to examine more closely the methods that might be used in estimating effect sizes.

ESTIMATING THE EFFECT SIZE

In chapter 1 it was noted that the exact effect size is usually unknown; if researchers knew precisely how treatment groups would differ, there would be little point in carrying out the research. There are three general methods that might be followed in estimating effect sizes in statistical power analysis. First, inductive methods might be used. If similar studies have been carried out before, results from these studies might be used to estimate effect sizes in new studies. Previously, this inductive method might have relied heavily on personal experience (i.e., whatever studies a particular researcher has read and remembers), but with the rapid growth of metanalysis it is often easy to find summaries of the results of large numbers of relevant studies (see, e.g., Lipsey & Wilson, 1993) already translated into a convenient effect size metric (e.g., d, r^2, or more generally, PV).

Second, deductive methods, in which existing theory or findings in related areas are used to estimate the size of an effect, might be used. For example, suppose researchers want to estimate the effect of vitamin supplements on performance in long distance races. Suppose further that they know that the vitamin supplement has a strong and immediate effect on the efficiency with which the body uses oxygen, and efficiency in using oxygen is strongly correlated with success in such a race. It seems reasonable in this context to deduce that the vitamin supplements should have a strong influence on race outcomes.

Third, researchers might use widely accepted conventions about what represents a large, medium, or small effect to structure a power analysis. As is noted later, analyses based on these conventions require very careful thought about what sort of effect is realistically expected or what sort of information about statistical power is really needed. Nevertheless, the use of these conventions can help researchers in carrying out useful and informative power analyses, even if there is no basis for predicting with any accuracy the size of the treatment effect.

Inductive Methods

Inductive methods are best where there is a wealth of relevant data. For example, there have been hundreds and perhaps thousands of studies on the validity of cognitive ability tests in predicting performance in school and on the job (J. E. Hunter & Hirsch, 1987; J. E. Hunter & R. F. Hunter, 1984). Similarly, Lipsey and Wilson (1993) reviewed numerous metanalyses of psychological and educational interventions. Nor is this method restricted to the behavioral and social sciences; metanalytic procedures are being applied in areas such as cancer research (e.g., Himel, Liberati, Gelber, & Chalmers, 1986); Lipsey and Wilson (1993) cited numerous metanalyses of research on other medical topics.

Suppose research was being done on the effectiveness of programs designed to help individuals quit smoking and there are sufficient resources to collect data from 250 subjects. Lipsey and Wilson (1993) cited two separate metanalyses that suggest relatively small effects on quit rates (for physician-delivered and worksite programs, $d = .34$ and $d = .20$, based on 8 and 20 studies, respectively). This body of research provides a reasonable starting point for estimating power; a weighted mean of these two d values is .24. The F equivalent for this effect size estimate, given a study comparing quit rates in a treatment group ($n = 125$) with those in a control group ($n = 125$) is $F(1, 248) = 3.57$. The power for testing the traditional null hypothesis ($\alpha = .05$) is therefore just below .50 (the F equivalent for power of .50 from the One-Stop F Table is 3.81). If you were testing the hypothesis that treatments accounted for 1% or less of the variance in outcomes in the population, power would be well below .50 (the F equivalent for power of .50 is 10.33; in this study, power is lower than .10).

Power is low even though the study has a relatively large sample ($N = 250$). This is true because the effects of smoking cessation programs on quit rates are small ($d = .24$ means that treatments account, on average, for about 1.4% of the variance in quit rates). The body of research in this area gives researchers good reason to expect small effects, and if they want to have adequate power for detecting these effects, they will need a much larger sample (e.g., you will need about

600 subjects to achieve a power of .80 in tests of the traditional null hypothesis).

Deductive Methods

Deductive methods are the best when there is a wealth of relevant theory or models; Newtonian mechanics is probably the best example of an area in which numerous effects can be deduced on the basis of a small set of theoretical statements and principles. However, there are areas in the social and behavioral sciences where the relevant theories or models are sufficiently well developed that sound inferences could be made about effect sizes. For example, the models most commonly used to describe human cognitive abilities are hierarchical in nature, with specific abilities linked to broad ability factors, which in turn are linked to a single general cognitive ability (see Carroll, 1993, for a review of factor-analytic studies). If researchers wanted to estimate the validity of a new test measuring specific abilities as a predictor of performance in school, they could use what is known about the structure of abilities to make a reasonable estimate; tests that are strongly related to verbal or to general cognitive ability factors are likely to show moderate to strong relations to school performance.

Suppose researchers used existing models of cognitive ability to estimate test validity and obtained a figure of .40 (i.e., estimated correlation between test scores and school performance). If they used a sample of 65 subjects, an expected correlation of .40 would yield an F equivalent value of $F(1, 62) = 11.80$, and the power for testing the traditional null would be greater than .80; tests of the hypothesis that tests account for more than 1% of the variance in the population would also have power of in excess of .80. Because the expected effect is relatively large, it is easy to obtain adequate power, even with a small sample.

Effect Size Conventions

As was noted in the preceding chapter, there are some widely accepted conventions for defining small, medium, and large effects. For example, a *small* treatment effect has been described as one in which treatments account for approximately 1% of the variance in outcomes, as one in which the difference between treatment and control group means is about two tenths of a standard deviation, or as one in which a person randomly selected from the treatment group has a probability of .56 of having a higher score than a person randomly selected from the control group (see Table 2.2). None of these figures is sacred or exact (e.g., 2% of the variance might reasonably be described as a small effect), but the conventions described in Table 2.2 do seem to be accepted as reasonable by many researchers, and they provide a basis for doing a power analysis even when the actual treatment effect cannot be estimated by inductive or deductive methods.

When conventions are used to estimate effect sizes, it is usually best to base a power analyses on small or small-to-medium effect sizes. As was noted in chapter 1, a study with sufficient power to detect a small effect will have sufficient power for detecting medium and large effects as well. If the study is planned with the assumption that the effect is a large one, there is considerable risk of missing meaningful effects that did not reach quite the magnitude researchers optimistically hoped to achieve. Thus, if the data and theory in a particular field do not provide a firm inductive or deductive basis for estimating effect sizes, researchers can always follow the convention and base their analysis on the assumption that the effects might very well be small. A study that has sufficient power to reliably detect small effects runs little risk of making a serious Type I or Type II error, regardless of the actual size of the treatment effect.[1]

FOUR APPLICATIONS
OF STATISTICAL POWER ANALYSIS

The two most common applications of statistical power analysis are in determining the power of a study, given N, ES, and α; and determining how many observations will be needed (i.e., N); given a desired level of power, an ES estimate, and an α value. Both of these analysis are extremely useful in planning research, and are usually so easy to do that they should be a routine part of designing a study. Power analysis may not be the only basis for determining whether to do a particular study or how many observations should be collected, but a few simple calculations are usually enough to help researchers make informed decisions in these areas. The lack of attention to power analysis (and the deplorable habit of placing too much weight on the results of small sample studies) are well documented in the research literature (J. Cohen, 1962; Haase, Waechter, & Solomon, 1982; Sedlmeier & Giger-

---

[1]As was noted in chapters 1 and 2, Type I errors are a concern only when there is some possibility that the null hypothesis is true, which is virtually never the case in tests of the traditional null. Type II errors are still possible if the treatment effect is extremely small, but this type of error (i.e., concluding that treatments have no effect when in fact they have a completely trivial effect) would not be regarded as very serious.

enzer, 1989), and there is no good excuse to ignore power in designing studies.

There are two other applications of power analysis that are less common, but no less informative. First, researchers can use power analysis to evaluate the sensitivity of studies. That is, power analysis can tell what sorts of effect sizes might be reliably detected in a study. If the effect of a treatment is expected to be small, it is important to know whether the study will detect that effect, or whether the study only has sufficient sensitivity to detect larger effects. Second, power analysis can be used to make rational decisions about the criteria used to define statistical significance.

Calculating Power

Chapters 1 and 2 were largely devoted to explaining the theory and procedures used in calculating the statistical power of a study, and all of these details are not repeated here. It is, however, useful to comment on problems or issues that arise in carrying out each of the steps of statistical power analysis.

As the examples presented in chapter 2 suggest, in estimating the level of power expected in a study researchers should do the following:

1. Estimate the size of the effect, expressed in terms of a common ES measure, such as PV or d.
2. Determine the degrees of freedom (i.e., v1 and v2) for the statistical test to be performed, and the type of hypothesis (e.g., traditional null, minimum-effect hypothesis) to be tested.
3. Translate that effect size estimate into an F equivalent, given these v1 and v2 values.
4. Use the One-Stop F Table to estimate power. If the F equivalent is greater than the F needed to obtain power of .80, there should be sufficient power for most purposes, and a more precise estimate is probably not necessary. If the F equivalent is smaller than the F needed to obtain power of .50, there will not be sufficient power for most purposes, and a more precise estimate is probably not helpful. If the F equivalent is between these two values on the One-Stop F Table, use the interpolation formula in chapter 2 (Equation 10) to estimate the power level of the study.

As was noted earlier, there are several ways to estimate the effect size. Regardless of the method chosen, it is usually better (or at least more prudent) to underestimate than to overestimate ES values; a study with enough power to detect a small effect will also have enough power to detect a larger effect. Second, when planning a study, some preliminary estimate of the sample size (and possibly of the research design) must be made. This estimate, which may be modified if the study yields either too much or too little power, helps in determining the degrees of freedom of the F statistic. In most cases, power analyses are likely to lead to increase the sample size, but it is certainly possible that a power analysis will lead to the conclusion that adequate power can be obtained with a smaller sample than the one initially planned.

As was emphasized in chapters 1 and 2, power depends substantially on the precise hypothesis being tested. It is easier to obtain high levels of power for tests of the traditional null hypothesis than for tests of a minimum-effect hypothesis, at least in part because the traditional null is so easily rejected. Tests of minimum-effect hypotheses, although more difficult, are also likely to be more informative.

Finally, it is necessary to make a decision about the significance criterion. The issues involved in making this choice are discussed later in this chapter. Here, it is sufficient to note that the choice is often practically limited to the conventional values of .05 versus .01. If any other value is used to define statistical significance (e.g., .02 might be a perfectly reasonable choice in some settings), it will be necessary to fight convention and defend the choice to a potentially hostile set of reviewers, readers, and editors.

Determining Sample Sizes

Rather than calculating the level of power a particular study had or will have, it is often useful to determine the sample or research design needed to achieve specific levels of power. To do this, first decide how much power is wanted. As noted in chapter 2, it is hard to justify a study design that yields power less than .50; when power is less than .50, the study is more likely to lead to an incorrect conclusion (i.e., it will not reject H_0, even though it is virtually certain this hypothesis is wrong) than to a correct one. Power substantially above .80 might be desirable, but it is often prohibitively difficult to obtain; in most analyses, the desirable level of power is likely to be .80.

Once the desirable level of power is determined, determining sample sizes follows the same general pattern as the determination of power itself. That is, the research design, the estimated effect size, the nature of the hypothesis being tested, and the significance criterion being used need to be considered. Table 3.1 can be used to determine sample sizes needed to detect a wide range of effects.

The rows of Table 3.1 correspond to effect sizes, described in terms of either the standardized mean difference (d) or the proportion of variance explained (PV), which represent the most common effect size

TABLE 3.1
V2 Needed for Power = .80 (α = .05) in Tests of Traditional Null Hypothesis

												$V1$						
ES	PV	d	1	2	3	4	5	6	7	8	9	10	12	15	20	30	40	60	120
.01	.20	775	952	1,072	1,165	1,260	1,331	1,394	1,451	1,504	1,580	1,670	1,825	1,992	2,302	2,565	3,027	4,016
.02	.29	385	473	533	579	627	662	694	722	762	787	832	909	993	1,176	1,313	1,513	2,010
.03	.35	255	313	353	384	416	439	460	479	505	522	552	603	660	782	874	1,008	1,341
.04	.41	190	233	263	286	310	328	343	358	377	390	413	451	494	585	654	774	1,031
.05	.46	151	186	209	228	247	261	273	285	300	310	329	359	402	466	522	618	825
.06	.51	125	154	173	189	204	216	227	236	249	257	273	298	333	388	434	514	687
.07	.55	106	131	148	161	174	184	193	204	212	220	233	255	285	331	371	440	601
.08	.59	92	114	128	140	152	160	168	178	185	191	203	222	248	289	324	384	525
.09	.63	81	100	113	124	134	142	149	157	164	169	179	196	220	256	287	341	466
.10	.67	73	90	101	110	120	127	133	141	146	152	161	176	197	230	258	312	419
.11	.70	66	81	91	101	108	115	120	127	132	137	148	159	178	208	238	283	388
.12	.74	60	74	83	92	99	104	110	116	121	125	135	145	163	190	218	259	355
.13	.77	55	68	76	84	90	96	101	106	111	115	124	133	150	178	200	238	327
.14	.81	50	62	70	78	83	88	94	98	102	106	114	123	138	165	185	220	302
.15	.84	47	58	65	72	77	82	87	91	95	98	106	115	129	153	172	205	286
.16	.87	43	54	61	67	72	76	81	85	88	92	99	107	120	143	161	192	268
.17	.91	40	50	57	63	68	72	76	80	83	86	93	101	112	134	151	183	251
.18	.94	38	47	53	59	63	67	71	75	78	81	87	96	106	126	142	172	236
.19	.97	36	44	50	55	59	63	67	70	73	77	82	90	101	119	136	163	227
.20	1.00	34	42	47	52	56	60	64	67	69	73	77	85	96	112	129	154	214
.22	1.06	30	37	42	47	51	54	57	60	62	65	70	76	86	102	116	139	194
.24	1.12	27	34	39	42	46	49	52	54	57	59	63	69	78	93	105	128	178
.26	1.19	25	31	35	38	42	44	47	49	52	54	58	63	71	85	96	117	163
.28	1.25	22	28	32	35	38	41	43	45	48	49	53	58	65	78	90	107	152
.30	1.31	21	26	30	32	35	37	40	42	44	45	49	53	61	72	83	100	142
.32	1.37	19	24	27	30	33	35	37	39	40	42	45	50	56	68	76	93	131
.34	1.44	18	22	25	28	30	32	34	36	38	39	42	46	52	63	72	87	123

estimates in the literature. Table 3.2 provides formulas for translating a number of other statistics, including F, into d and/or PV.

The values in Table 3.1 represent degrees of freedom (v2) rather than exact sample sizes (N). The reason for presenting a table of v2 values rather than presenting a table of sample sizes is that N is a function of both v1 and v2. In many applications $N = v1 + v2 + 1$, but in complex multifactor designs (e.g., studies using factorial ANOVA) the total sample size depends on the number of levels of all design factors, and without knowing the research design in advance, it is impossible to put together an accurate N needed table. In most cases, however, the sample size needed to achieve power of .80 will be very close to the v2 value shown in Table 3.1.

Table 3.1 presents v2 needed when testing the traditional null hypothesis. Table 3.3 presents the v2 needed when testing the hypothesis that treatments account for 1% or less of the population variance in outcomes. It becomes evident that larger samples are needed when testing this minimum-effect hypothesis than when testing the traditional (but sometimes trivial) hypothesis that treatments have no effect whatsoever.

To illustrate the use of Tables 3.1 and 3.3, consider a study comparing the effectiveness of four diets. Suppose researchers expect a small to moderate effect (e.g., the choice of diets is expected to

TABLE 3.2

Translating Common Statistics Into Standardized Mean Difference (d) or Percentage of Variance (PV) Values

Standardized Mean Difference (d)

$$d = \frac{2r}{\sqrt{1-r^2}}$$

$$d = \frac{2t}{\sqrt{v2}}$$

Percentage of Variance (PV)

$$PV = \frac{t^2}{t^2 + v2}$$

$$PV = \frac{v1F}{v1F + v2}$$

$$PV = \frac{d^2}{d^2 + 4}$$

TABLE 3.3
V2 Needed for Power = .80 (α = .05) in Tests of the Hypothesis That Treatments Account for 1% or Less of the Variance in Outcomes

ES									V1									
PV	d	1	2	3	4	5	6	7	8	9	10	12	15	20	30	40	60	120
.02	.29	3,225	3,242	3,301	3,266	3,334	3,349	3,364	3,429	3,442	3,454	3,479	3,570	3,621	3,900	4,042	4,379	5,260
.03	.35	1,058	1,086	1,104	1,122	1,139	1,176	1,185	1,199	1,212	1,254	1,271	1,303	1,377	1,518	1,615	1,833	2,299
.04	.41	573	590	607	623	650	658	670	683	694	716	736	779	836	920	993	1,151	1,458
.05	.46	373	389	405	422	434	445	457	472	483	492	509	541	586	652	728	833	1,075
.06	.51	269	285	299	313	323	334	343	357	365	373	387	414	450	506	568	654	854
.07	.55	208	223	235	246	255	267	275	283	290	297	315	338	362	419	460	533	718
.08	.59	166	180	192	202	211	219	226	236	243	249	265	279	307	357	393	457	606
.09	.63	139	151	161	170	180	187	193	199	208	214	224	241	266	303	343	400	532
.10	.67	117	130	139	147	154	162	168	174	179	187	196	212	234	268	297	355	473
.11	.70	101	113	122	129	136	143	149	154	159	166	174	189	205	240	266	318	426
.12	.74	89	99	108	115	121	127	133	138	142	147	157	170	185	217	241	289	388
.13	.77	80	89	97	104	109	114	121	125	129	133	142	152	168	197	220	264	355
.14	.81	72	80	87	94	99	104	110	114	118	121	130	139	154	181	202	243	327
.15	.84	65	73	80	86	91	95	101	105	108	112	120	128	142	168	187	225	303
.16	.87	59	67	73	79	84	88	93	97	100	103	111	119	132	156	174	209	283
.17	.91	54	61	68	73	77	81	85	90	93	96	103	110	123	145	162	195	269
.18	.94	49	57	63	68	72	76	79	83	86	89	96	103	115	136	152	183	252
.19	.97	45	53	58	63	67	71	74	78	81	84	90	97	108	127	144	172	238
.20	1.00	42	49	55	59	63	67	69	73	76	79	84	91	101	120	137	162	224
.22	1.06	37	43	48	52	56	59	62	65	68	70	75	81	91	107	123	146	204
.24	1.12	32	38	43	47	50	53	56	59	61	63	68	74	83	97	111	134	185
.26	1.19	29	34	38	42	45	48	51	53	55	57	61	67	75	90	101	122	169
.28	1.25	26	31	35	38	41	43	46	48	50	53	56	61	69	82	92	111	156
.30	1.31	24	28	32	35	37	40	42	44	46	48	51	56	63	75	86	103	144
.32	1.37	21	26	29	32	34	36	39	40	42	44	47	52	58	69	79	96	135
.34	1.44	20	24	27	30	32	34	36	37	39	41	44	48	54	64	73	89	125

account for about 5% of the variance in weight loss). To achieve power of .80 in testing the traditional null hypothesis (with α = .05), look down the column of Table 3.1 that corresponds to v1 = 3 (i.e., with four diets, there are three degrees of freedom) and find that the v2 needed for PV = .05 would be about 209. It would therefore be necessary to have a sample of about 213 subjects (i.e., N = 209 + 3 + 1) to achieve this level of power, or about 54 per group. Table 3.3 shows the v2 needed to achieve power of .80 in testing the hypothesis that treatments account for 1% or less of the variance in outcomes. To achieve a power of .80 in testing this minimum-effect hypothesis, a sample of about 409 (i.e., N = 405 + 3 + 1), or about 100 per group, is necessary. This sample is almost twice as large as the one needed to reject the traditional null hypothesis that treatments have no effect. However, if a study is put together that allows the rejection of the hypothesis that treatments have a negligibly small effect (e.g., they account for less than 1% of the variance in outcomes), researchers will not only know that treatments have some effect, but they will also have a formal test of the hypothesis that the effect is large enough to warrant attention.

Determining the Sensitivity of Studies

It is often useful to know what sort of effect could be reasonably detected in a particular study. If a study can reliably detect only a large effect (especially in a context where small effects are expected to actually occur), it might be better to postpone that study until the resources needed to obtain adequate power are available. The process of determining the effect size that can be detected given particular values for N and α, together with a desired level of power, again closely parallels the procedures already described. In fact, Tables 3.1 and 3.3, which specify the v2 needed to achieve power of .80 in testing both traditional and minimum-effect hypotheses, are also quite useful for determining the type of effect that could be reliably detected in a given study.

Suppose researchers are comparing two methods of mathematics instruction. There are 140 students available for testing (70 will be assigned to each method), and the researchers decide to use an α level of .05 in testing hypotheses. Here, v1 = 1 (i.e., if two treatments are compared, there is one degree of freedom for this comparison) and v2 = 138 (i.e., v2 = N - v1 - 1). If they look down the v1 = 1 column of Table 3.1, these researchers find that 138 falls somewhere between the v2 needed to detect the effect of treatments when PV = .05 and PV = .06 (or between d = .46 and d = .51). In other words, with 140 students, researchers would have power of .80 to detect a small to moderate effect, but they would not have this level of power for detecting a truly small (but perhaps important) effect.

Consider another example. Suppose there are four cancer treatments and 44 patients. Here, $v1 = 3$ and $v2 = 40$. Table 3.1 shows a power of .80 to detect effects that are quite large (i.e., $PV = .24$); if the true effects of treatments are small or even moderate, power to detect these effects will drop substantially.

Both of the previous examples are based on tests of the traditional null hypothesis. To test the hypothesis that treatments account for 1% or less of the variance in outcomes (which corresponds to d values of .20 or lower), the sample of 140 students will give a power of .80 for detecting differences this large between the two treatments only if the true effect is relatively large (i.e., $PV = .09$ or $d = .63$). This level of power will be available for detecting nontrivial differences among the four cancer treatments (with $N = 44$) only if the true differences between treatments are truly large (i.e., $PV = .24$).

Determining Appropriate Decision Criteria

As was noted earlier, the choice of criteria for defining statistical significance is often practically limited to the conventional values of .05 versus .01 (occasionally, social scientists use .001 or .10 as significance levels, but these are rare exceptions). The choice of any other value (e.g., .06) is likely to be met with some resistance, and the battle is probably not worth the effort. Because the choice among significance levels is constrained by convention, the steps involved in making this choice do not exactly parallel the processes laid out in the three preceding sections of this chapter. Rather than describing specific steps in choosing between .05 and .01 as alpha levels, the range of issues that are likely to be involved in making this choice are discussed. This discussion leads to the conclusion the .01 level should never be used when testing traditional null hypotheses, nor should other procedures designed to guard against Type I errors in testing this hypothesis be used. As is shown later, choice of the .01 significance criterion leads to a substantial reduction in statistical power, with virtually no meaningful gain in terms of protection against Type I errors. The same is true of most procedures designed to reduce Type I errors (See Zwick & Marascuilo, 1984, for a review of procedures used in testing multiple contrasts).

Balancing Risks in Choosing Significance Levels.   In chapter 1 it was noted that when testing the traditional null hypothesis, two types of errors are possible. Researchers who reject the null hypothesis when in fact it is true make a Type I error (α is the probability of making this error if H_0 is in fact true). The practical effect of a Type I error is that researchers could come to believe that treatments have some effect when in fact they have no effect whatsoever. Researchers who fail to reject the null hypothesis when it is false make a Type II error (β is the probability of making this error when H_0 is in fact false, and power = 1 - β). The practical effect of making a Type II error is that researchers might give up on treatments that in fact have some effect.

The most common strategy for reducing Type I errors is to make it difficult to reject the null hypothesis (e.g., by using .01 rather than .05 as a criterion for significance). Unfortunately, this strategy also substantially reduces the power of the tests. For example, suppose two treatments (with 200 people assigned to each treatment) are compared and a small effect (i.e., d = .20) is expected. Using .05 as a significance criterion, the power would be .51; if α = .01, power drops to .29 (J. Cohen, 1988). This tradeoff between Type I error protection and power suggests that in deciding which significance level to use, the risk and consequences of a Type I error must be balanced with the risk and consequences of a Type II error. Nagel and Neff (1977) discussed decision-theoretic strategies, choosing an alpha level that provides an optimum balance between the two errors.

Cascio and Zedeck (1983) suggested that Equation 1 can be used to estimate the apparent relative seriousness (*ARS*) of Type I versus Type II errors in statistical significance tests:

$$ARS = \frac{p(H_1)\beta}{\left[1 - p(H_1)\right]\alpha} \tag{11}$$

where:

$p(H_1)$ = probability that H_0 is false

According to Equation 1, if the probability that treatments have some effect is .7, alpha is .05, and the power is .80, then a mistaken rejection of the null hypothesis (i.e., a Type I error) is treated as if it was 9.33 times as serious [i.e., (.7 * .2)/(.3 * .05) = 9.33] as the failure to reject the null when it is wrong (i.e., a Type II error). In contrast, setting α at .10 leads to a ratio of 4.66, or to the conclusion that a Type I errors are treated as if they are 4.66 times as serious as a Type II error (See also Lipsey, 1990).

The first advantage of Equation 1 is that it makes explicit values and preferences that are usually not well understood, by either researchers or by consumers of social science research. In the scenario described earlier, an alpha level of .05 makes sense only if researchers think that Type I errors are over nine times as serious as Type II errors. If they believe that Type I errors are only four or five times as serious as Type II errors, the significance level should be set at .10, not at .05.

The second advantage of Equation 1 is that it explicitly involves the probability that the null hypothesis is true. As was noted in several other contexts, the traditional null hypothesis is virtually never true, which means that both null hypothesis testing and efforts to reduce Type I errors are sometimes pointless (Murphy, 1990). If the null hypothesis is by definition false, then it is not possible to make a Type I error. Thus, the only circumstance in which researchers should use stringent significance criteria, adopt testing procedures that minimize Type I errors, and so on are those in which the null hypothesis might actually be true. This virtually never happens when testing the traditional null hypothesis, but it might occur when testing a minimum-effect hypothesis.

Should Researchers Ever Worry About Type I Errors?   In testing the traditional null hypothesis, it is often virtually impossible to make a Type I error, no matter how hard researchers try. If H_0 is known to be false, there simply is no way to make a Type I error, and their only concern should be maximizing power (and therefore minimizing Type II errors). In contrast, there are good reasons for concern over Type I errors when testing a minimum-effect hypothesis. It is virtually impossible to devise serious treatments or interventions that have no effect whatsoever, but there are many treatments, interventions, tests, and so on. that have only negligible effects. If the hypothesis to be tested is that the effect of treatments falls under some sensible minimum, then it is quite possible that the null will be true, and they will in fact learn something by testing it.

As Equation 1 suggests, it is impossible to sensibly evaluate the relative emphasis given to Type I versus Type II errors unless the probability that the null hypothesis is in fact true can be estimated. Table 3.4 shows the relative seriousness with which Type I versus Type II errors are treated as a function of both the alpha rate and the probability that the null hypothesis is true in studies where power = .80. For example, if there is a 5% chance that treatments really do have a negligible effect (i.e., the probability that the minimum-effect null hypothesis is true is .05), the decision to use an alpha level of .01 makes sense only if researchers believe that Type I errors are 380 times as serious as Type II errors. As Table 3.4 indicates, as alpha increases (i.e., as it becomes easier to reject H_0), the relative seriousness attached to Type I versus Type II errors goes down. If they believe that Type II errors are at all serious relative to Type I errors, the message of Table 3.4 is clear—that is, researchers should use a more lenient criterion for determining statistical significance.

It is easy to rearrange the terms of Equation 1 to compute the alpha level that should be used to reach an appropriate balance between Type I and Type II errors, a balance described as the *desired relative seriousness (DRS)*.[2] For example, if researchers decided that they wanted to treat Type I errors as twice as serious as Type II errors, the desired relative seriousness is 2.00; if the probability that the null hypothesis was true was .30, power was .80, and they wanted to treat Type I errors as if they were twice as serious as Type II errors, an alpha level of .23 should be used. The desired alpha level (i.e., level that will yield the appropriate balance between Type I and Type II errors) can be obtained from Equation 2:

$$\alpha_{desired} = \left[\frac{p(H_1)\beta}{1 - p(H_1)} \right] \left(\frac{1}{DRS} \right) \tag{2}$$

where:

$\alpha_{desired}$ = alpha level that will yield the desired relative seriousness of Type I and Type II errors

DRS = desired relative seriousness of Type I and Type II errors

To repeat a critical point, researchers should be concerned with Type I errors if and only if there is a realistic possibility that such an error can occur. One of the distinctions between the traditional null

TABLE 3.4

Relative Seriousness of Type I versus Type II Errors as Function of Alpha and Probability that the Null Hypothesis is True (Power = .80)

Probability that	α		
H_0 is True	.01	.05	.10
.50	20.00	4.00	2.00
.30	46.66	9.33	4.66
.10	180.00	36.00	18.00
.05	380.00	76.00	38.00

[2]Keep in mind, however, that using nonconventional alpha levels will often require researchers to vigorously defend their choice, even in contexts where the conventional choice (e.g., .05, .01) makes no sense whatsoever.

and minimum-effect tests is that there is a realistic possibility that the minimum-effect null hypothesis will be true, which suggests that serious decisions must be made about the appropriate balance between Type I and Type II errors. Equations 1 and 2 can help you make those decisions.

CONCLUSIONS

Statistical power analysis can be used in planning future studies (e.g., determining how many subjects are needed) and/or in diagnosing studies that have already been carried out (e.g., calculation of power levels helps sensibly interpreting significance tests). All applications of statistical power analysis require at least an estimate of the true effect size; estimates can be obtained from literature reviews or relevant theory. Even where little is known about the true effects of treatments, effect size conventions can be used to structure power analyses.

It is possible to use the methods described here to determine the probability that a study will correctly reject the null hypothesis, determine the number of subjects or observations needed to achieve adequate power, determine the sort of effects that can be reliably detected in a particular study, or make informed choices about the criteria that define statistical significance. As has been noted throughout this book, these applications of power analysis are not in any way limited to tests of the traditional null hypothesis, but rather can be easily adapted to more interesting and informative tests of the hypothesis that treatment effects exceed some minimum level.

The distinction between traditional and minimum-effect hypotheses is especially important when making decisions about criteria for defining a significant outcome. Simply put, when testing the traditional null hypothesis, there is rarely any justification for choosing a stringent alpha level (e.g., .01 rather than .05). Procedures designed to protect against Type I errors (e.g., Bonferroni corrections) usually reduce power, and should only be applied if there is some realistic possibility that a Type I error can be made. This is unlikely when testing the traditional null hypothesis; this hypothesis is usually known to be incorrect, virtually by definition. Type I errors are a very real concern in tests of minimum-effect hypotheses, and the equations presented here allow researchers to rationally assess the relative emphasis placed on maximizing statistical power versus avoiding errors of this sort.

4

Illustrative Examples

The purpose of this chapter is to illustrate the application of power analysis. It uses real examples from the published literature to show how the methods described in this book can be applied to simple statistical tests as well as to more complex experiments and field studies. In particular, it shows how the One-Stop F Table, together with Tables 3.1 and 3.3, can be used to provide a range of useful information about research and help in planning and interpreting research in the behavioral and social sciences.

The chapter begins with an examination of two studies that used relatively simple statistical analyses (i.e., t tests and correlations), and shows how power analysis sheds light on the strengths and weaknesses, as well as the meaning of these studies. Next, it considers more complex statistical analyses, including factorial analyses of variance and multiple regression analysis, and shows how the tables developed in this book can be applied in analyzing these studies.

SIMPLE STATISTICAL TESTS

T Tests

Perhaps the most familiar statistical problem involves the comparison, via the t test, of the mean scores of subjects who do and do not receive some treatment. A research design in which subjects are randomly assigned to treatment and control conditions is very easy to implement and can provide very clear-cut and convincing answers to what are sometimes quite complex questions. To illustrate the many applications of statistical power analysis in studies employing this design, a study of the effects of regular exercise on placental growth rates in pregnant women (Clapp & Rizk, 1992) has been chosen.

Clapp and Rizk (1992) measured placental volumes in 18 healthy women who maintained a regular routine of exercise during pregnancy. Nine of the women engaged in aerobics, four ran, and five swam. The control group comprised 16 females who did not engage in such a regimen. Placental volumes were measured using modern ultrasound techniques at 16, 20, and 24 weeks gestation. Results of the study are reproduced in Table 4.1.

Two aspects of this study are especially noteworthy. First, the sample is small (i.e., $N = 34$). In most cases, this would mean very low power levels. However, in this study the effects are quite strong. In the three time periods studied, exercise accounted for between 29% and 47% of the variance in placental volume (d ranges from 1.71 to 2.41). Because the apparent effects of exercise were quite substantial, it should be easy to rule out the hypothesis that the treatment has no effect (traditional null), or even that the true effects of exercise are at best small (minimum-effect hypothesis).

Traditional versus Minimum-effect Tests. This t test has 32 degrees of freedom in this study; if it is squared, the statistic is distributed as F with 1 and 32 degrees of freedom. The One-Stop F Table shows entries for 1 and 30 and for 1 and 40 degrees of freedom, but none for 1 and 32 degrees of freedom, which means that researchers must interpolate to analyze these results. As can be seen in the One-Stop F Table, critical F values for the traditional null hypothesis at 1 and 30 degrees of freedom for $\alpha = .05$ and $\alpha = .01$ are 4.16 and 7.56, respectively. The corresponding values at 1 and 40 degrees of freedom are 4.08 and 7.31. Using Equation 9 in chapter 2, the $\alpha =$

TABLE 4.1

Placental Volumes Reported by Clapp and Rizk (1992)

Week	Control	Treatment	t	F	PV	d
	(N = 16)	(N = 18)				
16	106 (18)	141 (34)	3.68	13.55	.29	1.94
20	186 (46)	265 (67)	3.96	15.66	.33	1.71
24	270 (58)	410 (87)	5.45	29.66	.47	2.41

Note: Volumes are expressed in cm^3. Standard deviations are shown in parentheses. Note that in this table d represents the mean difference divided by the control group *SD*. Use of pooled *SD* values yields somewhat smaller d values, but they will nevertheless exceed conventional benchmarks for large effects.

.05 and $\alpha = .01$ critical values for 1 and 32 degrees of freedom when testing the traditional null hypothesis are 4.14 and 7.51, respectively. All of the observed F values in Table 4.1 are greater than 7.51, so the traditional null at the .01 level can be rejected and it may be concluded that regular exercise has some impact on placental volume.

The possibility that exercise has no effect can be conclusively ruled out, and the data suggest that the actual effect is quite large. However, it is always possible that the true effect is small, and the large PV and d values observed here represent chance fluctuations in a process that usually produces only a small effect. The One-Stop F table can be used to test the hypothesis that the effects of treatments are negligible, or perhaps small to moderate.

Again, using Equation 9 from chapter 2 to interpolate, the critical F ($\alpha = .05$) for the minimum-effect null hypothesis that the effect is small to medium in size (i.e., the null is that treatments account for no more than 5% of the variance in outcomes) is 9.52. All F values in Table 4.1 exceed 9.52, so the minimum-effect null hypothesis that the effects of treatments are no greater than small to moderate can be rejected, with a 95% level of confidence. This hypothesis can also be rejected at the .01 level for mean placental volumes at 20 and 24 weeks (critical $F = 15.26$; observed $F = 15.66$ and 29.44 at 20 and 24 weeks, respectively). That is, it is possible to be at least 99% confident that the effects of treatments exceed the definition of small to moderate.

Power Estimation. Assume, as the results of this study suggest, that the effects of maternal exercise on placental volume are substantial (e.g., exercise accounts for 25% of the variance in placental volume). If this assumption is true, then this study possesses very high levels of power for rejecting the traditional null. With 1 and 32 degrees of freedom, an effect size of $PV = .25$ has an F equivalent value of 10.66. The critical F for achieving a power of .80 at $\alpha = .05$ in this study is 8.3. The power to reject the hypothesis that treatments account for less than 1% of the variance in the population is also well in excess of .80; the critical F for power of .80 in testing this minimum-effect hypothesis is 10.12.

In addition to placental volume, Clapp and Rizk (1992) examined a range of other dependent variables for the women in this study. If exercise could function as a viable treatment of fetal under- or over-growth, it might be expected to have some effect on the final birthweight of the babies as well. In this case, Clapp and Rizk (1992) reported the mean birthweight of babies for women in the control group as 3,553gm ($SD = 309$) compared to 3,408 gm ($SD = 445$) for women in the treatment group. Reference to the One-Stop F Table shows that when testing hypotheses about birthweight, the traditional null hypothesis $[F(1, 32) = 1.19, p < .05]$ cannot be rejected.

One possible explanation for this finding is low power. If the true effect of exercise on birthweight (as opposed to placental volume) is small, power will be well below .50 in this study. For example, if it is assumed that the true effect of exercise on birthweight meets the conventional definition for a small effect (i.e., $PV = .01$), the F equivalent in this study is less than .32, whereas the critical F for a power of .50 to reject the traditional null at the .05 level is 4.03. Thus, the power of this study to detect traditionally significant differences in birthweight is much less than .50 (about .09 in fact). Of course, the power to detect substantively meaningful differences is even lower.

Sample Size Estimation.   How many subjects, then, would be required to reliably detect differences in birthweight as a result of exercise during pregnancy? In order to answer this question refer to Tables 3.1 and 3.3, which provide sample sizes needed, given that $\alpha = .05$ and the desired level of power is .80. If it is assumed that the effect of exercise on birthweight is small ($PV = .01$, $d = .20$), about 776 subjects in total (i.e., $N = v1 + v2$; for the t test, $v1 = 1$) or about 390 subjects in each group (i.e., 776/2) would be needed to achieve this level of power in tests of the traditional null hypothesis.

The power analyses conducted here suggest that the Clapp and Rizk (1992) study was well suited to answering questions about the effect of exercise on placental volume, which was its major focus. Power exceeded .80 for tests of both traditional and minimum-effect null hypotheses. However, the sample size is quite inadequate for answering questions about the effects of exercise on birthweight. Because a small effect might reasonably be expected here, huge samples are probably needed to provide adequate power.

Correlations

McDaniel (1988) used very large samples to study the validity measures of preemployment drug use as predictors of job suitability in the military. Validity coefficients for preemployment use of drugs such as marijuana, cocaine, various stimulants, and depressants were calculated in samples ranging in size from 9,224 to 9,355 subjects. As might be expected, the correlations were all statistically significant, and an incautious reading of these significance tests might mislead readers when arriving at conclusions about the value of these tests.

Several of the validities reported by McDaniel (1988) are shown in Table 4.2. These results are almost beyond the scope of the One-Stop F Table, but interpolating between v2 = 1,000 and v2 = 10,000 allows for the rejection of the traditional null hypothesis in every case at the .01 level. The interpolated critical F value for α = .01 and 9,224 degrees of freedom is 6.64, which is much smaller than any of these observed F values. However, as is noted later, the tests are significant because of the enormous samples involved, not because of the size of the effect.

Although significant in the traditional sense, McDaniel's (1988) validities are probably not meaningful in any substantive sense, and, as McDaniel himself noted, employers would be better advised to base their employment decision on information other than applicant's previous history of drug use. This study is an excellent example of the pitfalls of relying on tests of the traditional null hypothesis. These correlations are all significant, and it is all too easy to confuse "significant" with "meaningful." But, these correlations are so small that they should probably be ignored altogether.

Traditional versus Minimum-Effect Tests.   An examination of Table 4.2 shows just how small these validities are, accounting for less than half a percent of the variance in job suitability in each case. This fact is reflected in the One-Stop F Table as well. At 1 and 9,224 degrees of freedom, the interpolated critical F for rejecting the null hypothesis that the effect is negligibly small (i.e., 1% or less of the variance) is 126.1, well above any of the observed F values. In other words, none of the validities reaches the level designated as "trivial." Although they are significantly different from zero, it is clear that the relation between these tests and job suitability is so weak that the variables could be treated as virtually independent.

This example illustrates an important feature of minimum-effect null hypotheses. Unlike the traditional null, a minimum-effect null cannot necessarily be rejected simply by collecting more data. If an effect is genuinely negligible, it will always be negligible no matter how

TABLE 4.2
Predictive Validity of Preemployment Drug Use Reported by McDaniel (1988)

Drug	N	Validity	PV [a]	t	F
Marijuana	9,355	.07	.0049	6.79	46.06
Cocaine	9,224	.04	.0016	3.85	14.81
Stimulants	9,286	.07	.0049	6.76	45.73
Depressants	9,267	.07	.0049	6.76	45.63

- $_a$ - $PV = r^2$

many subjects are tested. This phenomenon is reflected in the One-Stop Table by the fact that critical F values for the 1% and 5% minimum-effect nulls do not asymptote as $v2$ increases. As $v2$ gets very large, the critical values for minimum-effect nulls keep pace with the increase and do not allow the rejection of the minimum-effect null hypothesis unless the effect is genuinely meaningful. Herein lies another important advantage of minimum-effect null hypothesis testing over traditional null hypothesis testing. When testing a minimum-effect null hypothesis, rejection cannot be guaranteed simply by collecting a large enough sample.

Power Estimation. As was noted earlier, the large samples employed in this study give tremendous power in tests of the traditional null hypothesis. If it is assumed that the relation between preemployment tests and job suitability is only half as large as the conventional definition of a small effect (i.e., $PV = .005$), there would still be power in excess of .80 for all of the tests reported in Table 4-2. With $N = 9,224$ and an assumed effect of $PV = .005$, the F equivalent is 46.35, whereas the critical F for achieving power of .80 is 7.81. It is little wonder that the author of this study (McDaniel, 1988) rejected the traditional null hypothesis. Even if the true effect is absolutely trivial, there is still plenty of power for rejecting the hypothesis that there is no effect whatsoever.

In contrast, if the hypothesis to be tested is that these tests account for 1% or less of the variance in suitability, McDaniel's study does not achieve power of even .50; to reach this level of power for samples this large, an F of over 120 is necessary. As was noted earlier, if the samples included 90,000 rather than 9,000 individuals, there still would not be power for rejecting a minimum-effect null with such data. The effect is much too small to be sensibly described as meaningful, and no matter how large the sample, it should still be small. The fact that the power needed to reject a minimum-effect hypothesis can never be attained when the effect is in fact negligible is neatly illustrated with this study.

STATISTICAL TESTS IN COMPLEX EXPERIMENTS

ANOVA

In a meticulously designed study, Martin, Mackenzie, Lovegrove, and McNicol (1993) examined the effect of tinted lenses on the reading performance of children with specific reading disabilities (SRDs). This treatment was first suggested by Irlen (1983), who distinguished a condition called "scotopic sensitivity syndrome" that could be ameliorated to some degree by prescription of lenses of certain tints. Controversy surrounds this treatment because it seems highly unlikely to many psychologists that filtering a few wavelengths from the perceptual array could have any impact on the higher cognitive processes associated with reading (B. J. Evans & Drasdo, 1991). Irlen (1983) proposed a mechanism involving perceptual distortions at certain wavelengths on the retina, but others (Cotton & K. M. Evans, 1990; Winter, 1987) have attributed any improvement in reading to placebo effects.

From an original sample of 300, Martin et al. (1993) selected 60 subjects for further study. Twenty subjects were normal readers, 20 were SRDs who could be treated by tinted lenses, and 20 were SRDs deemed unsuitable for the treatment. The sample selection controlled for such variables as native language, eyesight, intelligence, behavioral disorders, organic problems, and exposure to previous therapies. The three groups were compared on three occasions (pretest, posttest and follow-up) using the Neale Analysis of Reading Ability (Neale, 1973) which provided measures of reading accuracy and comprehension. A posttest occurred 1 year after the pretest and follow-up occurred 6 months after that. Although the sample in this study was small, the authors (Martin et al., 1993) were able to achieve substantial sensitivity because of their careful procedures and because they used a repeated measures design, in which multiple observations were obtained from each subject.

The data in this study were analyzed using a 3 x 3 analysis of variance. Martin et al. (1993) reported a significant main effect for groups on accuracy [$F(2, 57) = 65.57$] and comprehension [$F(2, 57) = 7.72$]. The main effect for occasion was also significant in each case [$F(2, 114) = 24.99$ for accuracy and $F(2, 114) = 36.43$ for comprehension]. The One-Stop F Table contains a range of useful information that helps put these results in perspective.

Power Estimation: Main Effects. There are good reasons to believe that the main effects in this study are large, and if this is true, the power of all main effect tests was extremely high. For the groups main effect the critical F value for achieving power of .80 to reject the traditional null ($\alpha = .05$) is 5.06. The F equivalent for a large effect in this study is 9.50, suggesting power well in excess of .80. Power was also greater than .80 for rejecting (at the .05 level) the minimum-effect null hypothesis that main effects account for 1% or less of the variance in treatments. Here, the critical F value was 6.19. In fact, in tests of the group's main effect, there would be power in excess of .80 for tests of the minimum-effect null for a small to medium effect (i.e., that treatments account for less than 5% of the variance in the population; the critical $F = 9.49$).

The same conclusions can be drawn about the occasions main effect. In this case, the critical F value for achieving power of .80 to reject the 1% minimum-effect null hypothesis at the.05 level was 6.96; for tests of the 5% minimum-effect null, the critical value is 12.72. With $v1 = 2$ and $v2 = 114$, a large effect (i.e., $PV = .25$) yields an F equivalent value of 19.00, which is well in excess of the critical F needed to attain power of .80 for tests of the minimum-effect null hypotheses described earlier.

Testing Interaction Hypotheses.   Examination of the main effects does not really address the principal research question (i.e., the effects of tinted lenses on reading performance of children with SRDs). If tinted lenses work, researchers should observe performance of the treated SRDs to be more similar to the untreated SRDs in the pretest condition but more similar to the subjects without reading disorders during posttest, hopefully persisting until follow-up. This is an interaction hypothesis. The interaction of groups by occasion was significant in the traditional sense for accuracy [F (4, 114) = 2.98] and comprehension [F (4, 114) = 3.13]. In both cases, the critical F (α = .05) value was 2.45 for tests of the traditional null. Researchers can also reject the a minimum-effect null (i.e., that the interaction effect accounts for 1% or less of the variance: critical $F = 3.01$) for comprehension measures.

The power of tests of these interactions can be determined from the One-Stop F Table. Suppose, for example, that the interaction effect is moderately large. If the population $PV = .10$, the F equivalent for v1 = 4, v2 = 114 is 3.16. The corresponding critical value for a power of .80 is 3.07. Power to reject the 1% minimum-effect null is somewhat lower. In this case, critical F values are 2.27 and 3.90 for power levels of .5 and .8, respectively. The F equivalent for a moderate effect (i.e., $PV = .10$) falls between these critical values, so Equation 10 (chap. 2) can be used to obtain a more accurate estimate. The power to reject the 1% minimum-effect null is approximately .5 + .3 (3.16 - 2.27) / (3.90 - 2.27) = .66. Thus, although acceptable for testing the traditional null hypothesis, this study is not quite adequate for addressing minimum-effect null hypotheses.

There is a reasonable level of power for detecting moderately strong interactions. Suppose, however, that the interaction effect is small (e.g., $PV = .01$). With $v1 = 4$ and $v2 = 114$, the equivalent F value is now .287, which is obviously too small to yield even marginal levels of power. In other words, the sample in this study is large enough to give adequate power if and only if the true interaction is at least moderately strong.

In a complex experiment, each statistical test may show a different level of power. First, the predicted and/or actual effect sizes may differ for main effects, simple interactions, and higher order interactions. Second, the degrees of freedom for different tests in a model may vary, sometimes substantially. In general, researchers are most likely to have higher power for testing main effects and lower power for testing complex interactions. First, main effects usually have more degrees of freedom. Second, main effects are usually (but not always) stronger than complex interactions. When the focus of the study is a complex three- or four-way interaction, very large samples might be needed to provide adequate power.

Martin et al. (1993) concluded that tinted lenses have no effect on reading ability, but the significant interactions just discussed do not warrant such a conclusion. The comprehension interaction, in particular, shows that treated SRDs performed like untreated SRDs in the pretest but improved to almost the same level as normals in the posttest and follow up, after lenses were applied.

Potential Difficulties in Estimating Power in Repeated Measures Designs. This study involved obtaining multiple measures from each of several subjects, and both hypothesis testing and power analysis in repeated measures designs can be complicated, because these designs lead to violations of important statistical assumptions that underlie the analysis of variance. In particular, research designs that involve obtaining multiple measures from each respondent can lead to violations of assumptions of independence of sphericity (i.e., the assumption that the variances of the differences between all possible pairs of repeated measures are equal). To obtain accurate results in such designs, both the degrees of freedom and the estimate of the noncentrality parameter must be adjusted by a factor ϵ (epsilon), which reflects the severity of violations of the assumption of sphericity (e.g., a good estimate of λ in repeated measures designs is given by $\epsilon * v2 * PV/(1 - PV)$; see Algina & Keselman, 1997, for discussions of sphericity and power).[1] However, this correction factor is not always reported, and cannot usually be calculated on the basis of results likely

---

[1]As the effect size increases (i.e., as *PV* get larger), this approximation becomes less accurate. However, for *PV* values of .30 or smaller, the results obtained by simply multiplying both degrees of freedom and *PV* values by ϵ are sufficiently accurate for the purpose of power analysis. As was noted in chapter 2, the sensible application of power analysis does not depend on accuracy to the second decimal place, and in most cases simple approximations will provide the information needed to estimate statistical power.

to be reported in a journal article.

A conservative approach to this problem is to make a worst-case correction (Greenhouse & Geisser, 1959). The factor epsilon ranges in value from a maximum of 1.0 (indicating no violation) to a minimum of

$$\epsilon = 1/(k - 1)$$

where:

k = number of levels of the repeated measures factor

When the degrees of freedom for factors involving repeated measures are multiplied by ϵ, it is possible to obtain a conservative test of significance by comparing the obtained F to the critical value of F using the epsilon-adjusted degrees of freedom.

For example, in this study, data are collected from each subject on three occasions, meaning that Occasion is a repeated-measures factor, and the Group x Occasion factor has a repeated measures component. The worst-case estimate of epsilon is that $\epsilon = .5$ [i.e, $\epsilon = 1/(3 - 1)$]. To use this worst-case estimate of epsilon here, multiply the degrees of freedom for the Occasion effect and the Occasion x Group effects by .5 (i.e., you would use degrees of freedom of $v1 = 1$, $v2 = 57$, and $v1 = 2$, $v2 = 114$, respectively, to test the Occasion and Occasion x Group effects rather than the actual degrees of freedom of $v1 = 2$, $v2 = 57$, and $v1 = 4$, $v2 = 114$). Similarly, it would be necessary to adjust the estimate of λ, also multiplying the estimate of λ by .5.

In practice, a good estimate of power can be obtained by simply multiplying both the degrees of freedom and PV by this worst-case estimate of ϵ (rather than directly adjusting your estimate of l (rather than directly adjusting your estimate of λ). A comparison of the power estimate obtained without any epsilon correction (the power estimates in this example did not include any correction for violations of the sphericity assumption) with the power estimate obtained making a worst-case assumption about violations provides a pretty good idea of the range of power values that could be reasonably expected.

Multiple Regression

Bunce and West (1995) examined the role of personality factors (propensity to innovate, rule independence, intrinsic job motivation) and group climate factors (support for innovation, shared vision, task orientation, participation in decision-making) in explaining innovation among health service workers. They carried out a 17-month, three-stage longitudinal study, and like most longitudinal studies, suffered

TABLE 4.3
Hierarchical Regression Results Reported in Bunce and West (1995)

Predictor	R^2	df	F	ΔR^2	df	F
Innovation—Stage 1	.18	1,75	16.73*			
Personality	.33	4,72	8.86*	.15	3,72	5.37*
Group Climate	.39	8,68	5.38*	.06	4,68	1.67

* $p < .05$ in tests of the traditional null hypothesis

significant loss of data (subject mortality) across time. Their N dropped from 435 at stage 1 to 281 and 148 at stages 2 and 3. Incomplete data reduced the effective sample size for several analyses further; several critical analyses appear to be based on a set of 76 respondents.

One analysis used stage 1 innovation, personality factors, and group factors as predictors in a hierarchical regression model, where the dependent variable was innovation at stage 2. The results of this analysis are summarized in Table 4.3.

The principal hypotheses tested in this analysis were that personality accounts for variance in stage 2 innovation not explained by innovation at stage 1, and group climate accounts for additional variance not accounted for by personality and stage 1 innovation. Because stage 1 innovation is entered first in the equation, researchers might interpret tests of the changes in R^2 as personality and climate are added to the equation as reflecting the influence of these factors on changes in innovation over time. The results suggest that personality has a significant effect, but that group climate does not account for variance above and beyond stage 1 innovation and personality.

Power Estimation. The results in Table 4.3 show a pattern we have encountered in some of the previous examples, a relatively small sample combined with some relatively large effects (e.g., stage 1 innovation accounts for 30% of the variance in stage 2 innovation), which makes it difficult to determine offhand whether or not the study will have enough power for its stated purpose. Some quick calculations suggest that it does not posses sufficient power to test all of the hypotheses of interest.

Rather than starting from the reported R^2 and F values, suppose researchers used standard conventions for describing large, medium, and small effects to structure their power analysis. In hierarchical regression studies, the predictors are usually chosen to be relevant to the dependent variable (which means they should each be related to Y), and are therefore usually also intercorrelated (i.e., several variables related to Y are likely to also be related to one another). As a result, they will generally find that the first variable entered will yield a relatively large R^2, and R^2 will go down as more variables are entered (J. Cohen & P. Cohen, 1983). This might lead to the expectation of a large effect for the first variable entered, a smaller R^2 for the next variable, and a small R^2 for the last variable. In chapter 2, it was noted that R^2 values of .25, .10, and .01 corresponded to conventional definitions of large, medium, and small effects (See Table 2.2). These values turn out to be reasonably similar to the actual R^2 and ΔR^2 values shown in Table 4.3 (i.e., .18, .15, and .06, respectively). Even more to the point, the overall R^2 , which represents the sum of these conventional values (i.e., $R^2 = .36 = .25 + .10 + .01$), is very similar to the actual overall value (i.e., $R^2 = .39$) reported by Bunce and West (1995).

To estimate power for detecting R^2 values of .25, .10, and .01, given the degrees of freedom in this study, the R^2 values must first be translated into F equivalents, using equations shown in Table 2-1. The F equivalents are 25.0, 3.60, and .76, respectively. There is plenty of power for testing the hypothesis that $R^2 = .25$ [$F(1, 75) = 25.0$]; the critical tabled F for this level of power is 8.01. Even when testing the minimum-effect hypothesis that the first variable entered accounts for 5% or less of the variance, power far exceeds .80.

There is also a reasonable level of power for testing the hypothesis that the second variable entered into the regression equation will have a medium effect [i.e., $R^2 = .10$, $F(3, 72) = 3.61$]. Interpolating between values in the One-Stop F Table, a power of .80 with an F value of 3.79 would be achieved. The F here is quite close, and the power of this test is approximately .78.

If it is assumed that the third in a set of intercorrelated predictors will generally yield a small increment in R^2 (i.e., $\Delta R^2 = .01$), then there is clearly not enough power to test that hypothesis. To achieve power of .50, an F of 1.69 would be necessary; assuming a small effect here, F is only .76.

The conclusions reached by looking at these three conventional values closely mirror those that would be obtained if the actual R^2 values were used. The F values for the first predictor (stage 1 innovation), second predictor (personality), and third predictor (group climate) are 16.73, 5.37, and 1.67, respectively. Power easily exceeds .80 in tests of the hypothesis that stage 1 innovation is related to stage 2 innovation (the critical F for this level of power is 8.01). Power also exceeds .80 for testing the hypothesis that personality accounts for variance not explained by stage 1 innovation (the critical F is 3.79; the observed F is 5.37). Power is just below .50 for testing the hypothesis that group climate accounts for variance not accounted for by the other two predictors (the critical F is 1.69; the observed F is 1.67).

Sample Size Estimation. The sample is certainly large enough to provide a powerful test of the hypothesis that stage 1 innovation predicts stage 2 innovation. Power is also reasonably high for testing the hypothesis that adding personality to the equation yields a significant increase in R^2. However, a much larger sample would be needed to provide a powerful test of the last hypothesis (i.e., that group climate explains additional variance).

Looking down the $v1 = 4$ column of the One-Stop F Table, it can be found that even when $v2 = 10,000$, the critical F value needed to have power of .80 is larger than 1.67. If researchers are seriously interested in pursuing hypotheses of this sort, truly enormous samples are necessary.

CONCLUSIONS

This chapter has provided numerous illustrations of how power analysis can be used to help design and interpret research studies. In particular, use of the One-Stop F Table in interpreting existing studies was demonstrated. The use of Tables 3.1 and 3.3 in estimating sample sizes required to achieve desired levels of power was also illustrated.

The chapter began by looking at a small sample study of the effects of exercise during pregnancy and noted that the study was adequate for answering questions about some dependent variables (due to the large effect of exercise), but inadequate for answering questions about dependent variables where a small or even moderate effect might be expected. Next, it looked at a large sample study of the effect of preemployment drug use on job suitability and noted that, although statistically significant, the effects were trivially small. The futility of trying to interpret such results was also noted.

A tightly controlled study of the effect of tinted lenses on the reading performance of children with specific reading disabilities was used to illustrate the applications of statistical power analysis in a complex ANOVA. It was lamented that power analytic information was not reported, especially given that they really wanted to accept the null hypothesis (i.e., that using the lenses has no real effect). Trends in the data were identified that were inconsistent with their conclusions, and suggested that the use of procedures designed to control for Type I errors may have caused more problems than they could possibly have solved.

Finally, the use of statistical power analysis was illustrated in a study that employed hierarchical regression techniques. This study examined the role of individual and group factors in influencing innovation; it was suggested that group factors made no independent contribution to the prediction of innovation. The analysis suggests that the study had woefully inadequate power for that purpose, and further that very large samples would be needed to provide adequate power. As a result, the failure to reject the traditional null hypothesis cannot be taken as evidence one way or another about the incremental effects of group climate on innovation.

5

The Implications of Power Analyses

The power of a statistical test is the probability that researchers will reject the null hypothesis being tested, given that this null hypothesis is in fact wrong. As has been noted throughout, the traditional null hypothesis that treatments have no effect whatsoever (or that the correlation between two variables is precisely zero, or any other hypothesis of "no effect") is very often wrong, and in this context the statistical power of a test is essentially the probability that the test will lead to the correct conclusion. When testing the traditional null hypothesis, it is obvious that power should always be as high as possible. When testing a minimum-effect hypothesis (e.g., that the effect of treatments is negligibly small, but not necessarily precisely zero), the implications of varying levels of statistical power are potentially more complex, and a wider range of issues needs to be considered in determining how to use and interpret statistical power analysis.

This chapter begins with a discussion of the implications of statistical power analysis for tests of both traditional and minimum-effect null hypotheses. Next, the benefits of taking statistical power seriously are discussed. Some of these are direct and obvious (e.g., if a power analysis is done, researchers are less likely to conduct a study in which the odds of failure substantially outweigh the odds of success), but there are also a number of indirect benefits to doing power analyses that may, in the long run, be even more important than the direct benefits. Finally, the question of whether power analysis renders the whole exercise of testing the traditional null hypothesis moot is considered. If power is very high (or very low), then the outcome of most statistical tests is not really in doubt, and the information from these tests might be severely limited as power reaches either extreme.

TESTS OF THE TRADITIONAL NULL HYPOTHESIS

Chapter 1 noted that two types of errors might be possible in testing statistical hypotheses. First, the null hypothesis might be rejected when it is in fact true (a Type I error). Second, the null hypothesis might fail to be rejected when it is in fact wrong (a Type II error). Textbooks invariably stress the need to balance one type of error against the other (e.g., procedures that minimize Type I errors also lead to low levels of power), but when the null hypothesis is known to be wrong, or when the probability that it is wrong is extremely high, there is little to be gained and much to be lost by attempting to maintain such a "balance" (Murphy, 1990).

The fact that the traditional null hypothesis is virtually always wrong leads to three conclusions about statistical power: Researchers cannot have too much power, they should take the simplest and most painless route to maximizing power, and tests with insufficient power should never be done.

You Cannot Have Too Much Power

If the null hypothesis is wrong, researchers cannot make a Type I error, and the only possible way they can make an error in statistical hypothesis testing is to fail to reject H_0. The reason for repeating this point so many times is that it flies in the face of convention, where substantial attention is often devoted to the highly unlikely possibility that a Type I error might occur. In tests of the traditional null, power is essentially the probability that the test will reach the right conclusion (because the traditional null is almost certainly wrong), and there is no conceivable reason why power should not be high. There are many practical problems with attaining high levels of power, as is noted later. However, it is always to researchers' advantage to maximize power in tests of the traditional null hypothesis.

Maximizing Power: The Hard Way and the Easy Way

There are two practical and eminently sensible ways to attain high levels of power. The easy way is to change the alpha level. As was pointed out in chapters 2 and 3, power is higher when a relatively lenient alpha level is used. Traditionally, the choice of criteria for defining statistical significance has been between alpha levels of .05

and .01. When testing the traditional null, there is little scientific or statistical advantage to using a stringent test, and the alpha level for tests should generally be set as high as possible. Unfortunately, there is likely to be resistance if alpha levels of .10, .20, or anything other than .05 or some other conventional figure is used, but this resistance is misplaced. Higher alpha rates yield more power, often with no meaningful increase in the likelihood of a Type I error.

The second strategy for maximizing power is to increase the sensitivity of the study, which generally implies using larger samples. Even though this strategy is more demanding than simply changing the alpha level, it is strongly recommended. Large, carefully constructed samples increase the generalizability and stability of findings, and they decrease the possibility that sampling error will lead to meaningless or misleading results. More is said about this in the sections that follow.

Although it is clearly harder to increase power by increasing N than by increasing α, this strategy has the immense benefit of improving your study. Simply changing the alpha level does nothing to enhance the meaningfulness or interpretability of your research, but the use of large samples helps to minimize one of the recurring problems in social science research—the overreliance on the unstable results obtained in small samples (Schmidt, 1992).

Tests with Insufficient Power Should Never Be Done

Suppose an individual was diagnosed with an ulcer, and the doctor talked about a new treatment. This treatment is more likely to make things worse than to make things better, and there are alternative treatments available that do not have this problem. Would this person take the new treatment? The answer is "no," and this analogy applies exactly to statistical tests of the traditional null hypothesis. If power is low, then a test of the traditional null hypothesis should not be carried out.

When power is less than .50 and researchers are certain (or virtually certain) that H_0 is wrong, the test is more likely to yield a wrong answer than a right one. More to the point, the test cannot possibly produce new and useful knowledge; it can only be misleading. If they were certain before the test that H_0 is false, then a test that rejects H_0 does not tell anything that is not already known. A test that fails to reject H_0 should not change anyone's mind either (if H_0 is wrong by definition, the results of the test will not change this), but people will sometimes be mislead by their data. Low power tests are unlikely to have any effect except to mislead and confuse researchers and readers.

TESTS OF MINIMUM-EFFECT HYPOTHESES

The alternative to testing the traditional null hypothesis that treatments have no effect is to test the minimum-effect null hypothesis that the effect of treatments is so small that it could be safely ignored. Different disciplines or research areas might require substantially different operational definitions of a "negligibly small" effect, and the standards suggested in previous chapters and in the One-Stop F Table (i.e., treatments accounting for less that 1%, or in some cases less than 5% of the variance in outcomes have negligibly small effects) will not always apply. Nevertheless, tests of minimum-effect null hypotheses are necessary if the whole enterprise of statistical hypothesis testing is to prove useful.

Statistical power analysis can be used to its fullest advantage in tests of minimum-effect null hypotheses. Because the hypothesis being tested may very well be true, it becomes important to develop specific procedures and criteria for "accepting the null," or determining when the evidence is consistent or inconsistent with the proposition that the effects of a particular treatment are indeed negligible; power analysis is extremely useful for this purpose. It also becomes important to give serious consideration to an issue that is usually (and incorrectly) presented in the context of traditional null hypothesis tests (i.e., the appropriate balance between Type I and Type II errors).

Accepting the Null

In traditional null hypothesis testing, the idea of accepting the null hypothesis is sometimes treated as a sort of heresy. Rather than allowing someone to accept the hypothesis that treatments have no effect, the traditional framework usually leaves two options: deciding there is sufficient evidence to reject the null (i.e., a significant outcome) and deciding there is not yet enough evidence to reject the null (i.e., a nonsignificant result). Because it is already known that the traditional null is false, the fact that enough evidence has not yet accumulated to confirm this fact tells more about the study than about the substantive phenomenon being studied.

As has been noted throughout, power is substantially affected by the size of the sample. If N is very small, researchers will not reject the null, no matter what research question they are pursuing. If N is large enough, the traditional null will be rejected, again no matter what research questions are being pursued. It is hard to resist the conclusion that tests of the traditional null hypothesis are little more than indirect measures of the sample size! In tests of the traditional null, the most logical interpretation of a nonsignificant result is that the sample is too small.

Occasionally, the door is left open for treating nonsignificant results as meaningful. For example, some journals allow for the possibility of publishing nonsignificant results, at least under some conditions (e.g., the inaugural issue of *Human Performance* included an editorial suggesting that nonsignificant results would be treated as meaningful if specific research design criteria, including a demonstration of adequate statistical power, were met). The argument sometimes offered purports that if well-designed studies fail to detect an effect, this might provide some evidence that the effect is likely to be a very small one, and the null hypothesis might be very close to being true, even if the effect of treatments is not precisely zero. Recently, Bayesian approaches have been applied to the problem of statistically demonstrating that an effect is so small that it should be effectively ignored (Rouanet, 1996). Nevertheless, the bias against accepting the null runs so strong in tests of the traditional null hypothesis that this framework simply does not leave any appealing alternative when the effect of treatments is negligibly small. Either a very large sample will be collected and the null will be rejected (which may mislead researchers into thinking that the effect of treatments is something other than trivial) or there will be a failure to reject it and researchers may go out and collect more data about an essentially meaningless question.

In tests of minimum-effect hypotheses, there is a realistic possibility that the hypothesis being tested (e.g., that the effect of treatments is at best negligible) is indeed true, and there is a real need to develop procedures of conventions for deciding when to accept the null. It is put forth here that power analysis plays a critical role in determining and defining those procedures or conventions.

Suppose the hypothesis being tested is that the effect of treatments is at best negligible (e.g., treatments account for 1% or less of the variance in outcomes). A powerful study could provide strong evidence that this hypothesis is in fact true. For example, if power is .80, this translates into odds of 4 to 1 that a statistical test will reject this hypothesis if it is in fact false. Failure to reject the null under these conditions can mean only one of two things: The null really is true; or the null is false, and this is that one test in five that yields the wrong result. The most logical conclusion to reach in this study is that the effects are negligibly small.

As was noted in chapter 3, a complete evaluation of the meaning of the outcomes of statistical tests requires some knowledge about the probability that the null hypothesis being tested actually is true (i.e., the prior probability of H_0). The central weakness of traditional null hypothesis testing is that this prior probability is thought or defined to be vanishingly small, and perhaps zero (Murphy, 1990). If researchers truly believe that the traditional null hypothesis is always wrong, there is little gained by testing it.

The central weakness of the alternative approach described in this book in which minimum-effect hypotheses are framed and tested is that this prior probability is generally unknown. In chapter 3, it was noted that the prior probability of the traditional null hypothesis would necessarily be very low, and, by most definitions, is exactly zero. It is likely that the prior probability of a minimum-effect null will also be somewhat low, especially if the hypothesis being tested is that the effect of treatments is at best negligible. The rationale for believing that this prior will be small is that most treatments in the social and behavioral sciences do indeed have an effect. Chapter 1 noted Lipsey and Wilson's (1993) review of over 300 metanalyses of research studying the efficacy of psychological, educational, and behavioral treatments. These metanalyses, in turn, summarize the results of thousands of studies in areas ranging from smoking cessation success rates to the effectiveness of computer-aided instruction. Over 85% of the metanalyses they summarized reported effects that exceeded conventional criteria for "small effects" (i.e., $d = .20$ or $PV = .01$ or less). It is clear from the massive body of research summarized that a broad range of treatments and applications in the social and behavioral sciences have at least some effect, and the likelihood that a new treatment will have an absolutely negligible effect seems small, especially if the new treatment is solidly based in theory and research.

Balancing Errors in Testing Minimum-Effect Hypotheses

In tests of the traditional null hypothesis, Type I errors are practically impossible and there is virtually nothing to be lost by setting alpha as high as possible. In tests of the minimum-effect hypothesis, the strategy of setting alpha as high as possible is no longer appropriate. The whole distinction between traditional and minimum-effect null hypotheses is that there is some realistic possibility that a minimum-effect null is true, and it is therefore possible to make a Type I error.

Although Type I errors are a real possibility in tests of minimum-effect null hypotheses, this does not mean that power should be ignored in carrying out these tests. The possibility of Type I errors should not blind researchers to the substantial likelihood that they will make Type II errors if they choose an unduly stringent alpha level. Choose any cell of the One-Stop F Table in Appendix B, and it becomes evident that: a larger F value is needed to reject the a minimum-effect null than to reject the traditional null, given the same alpha level; and a larger F value is needed to reject the hypothesis that effects are small to moderate (e.g., they account for 5% or less of the variance) than to reject the hypothesis that these effects are negligibly small (i.e., they account for 1% or less of the variance). That is, all other things being equal, it is harder to reject a minimum-effect hypothesis than to reject the hypothesis that treatments have no effect whatsoever. The more demanding the hypothesis (e.g., 5% vs. 1% as the upper bound to be tested), the harder it is to reject H_0. In light of all this, there is usually no good reason to make things even more difficult than they already are by choosing an unrealistically stringent alpha level. Earlier, it was suggested that when testing the traditional null hypothesis, the .01 level should usually be avoided. The same advice holds for tests of minimum-effect hypothesis; the .01 alpha level should still be avoided in most cases.

A two-part test is suggested for determining whether an alpha level of .01 rather than .05 should be used. First, .01 makes sense only if the consequences of a Type I error are relatively serious. Chapter 3 discussed concrete ways of comparing the perceived seriousness of Type I and Type II errors, and noted that researchers often act as if falsely rejecting the null is much more serious than failing to reject the null when necessary. This may well be true in some settings, but before deciding to set a stringent alpha level (thus markedly decreasing power), explicitly consider the relative costs of the two errors. Choose .01 only if there is a good reason to believe that a Type I error is substantially more serious than a Type II error.

Second, .01 makes sense only if the prior probability that the null hypothesis is true is reasonably high. That is, if the hypothesis to be tested is that a treatment has at most a negligible effect (e.g., it accounts for 1% or less of the variance in outcomes), then researchers should be concerned with Type I errors only if there is some realistic possibility that the effects of treatments are indeed trivial. Finally, keep in mind that this is a two-part test. Use the .01 level rather than the .05 level only if the consequences of a Type I error are large and the possibility that one might actually occur are substantial. In all other cases, use .05 as an alpha level, and use an even more lenient alpha level whenever possible.

POWER ANALYSIS: BENEFITS, COSTS, AND IMPLICATIONS FOR HYPOTHESIS TESTING

If power analysis is taken seriously, there will be fundamental changes in the design, execution, and interpretation of research in the social and behavioral sciences. Most of these changes will be beneficial, and are enthusiastic advocates of power analysis. As is noted later, the indirect benefits of power analysis may prove, in the long run, even more important than the direct benefits of adopting this approach. There are, of course, some costs associated with incorporating power analysis in the design and interpretation of research; however, the benefits still substantially outweigh the costs. Finally, it is useful to consider the implications of having extreme levels of power (either extremely high or extremely low) when conducting statistical hypothesis tests.

Direct Benefits of Power Analysis

As noted in chapter 1, power analysis can be used as both a planning tool (e.g., determining how many subjects should be included in a study) and a diagnostic tool (e.g., making sense out of previous studies that have either reported or failed to report significant results). Individuals who incorporate statistical power analysis into their research repertoire are better equipped to both plan and diagnose research studies, and they directly benefit from the information provided by power analyses.

Planning Research. Statistical power analysis provides a rational framework for making important decisions about the design and scope of a study. To be sure, there are many subjective decisions that must be made in applying power analysis (e.g., what effect size is anticipated, what alpha level is best), and the techniques described in this book do not represent a foolproof formula for making decisions about research design (e.g., choosing between repeated measures or between subjects designs) or sample size. The advantage of power analysis over other methods of making these important decisions, which are often made on the basis of force of habit or by following the lead of other researchers, is that it makes explicit the consequences of these design choices for the study. If researchers are seriously interested in rejecting the null hypothesis, a power analysis is absolutely necessary in making good choices about study design and sample size.

Power analysis also highlights the importance of a decision that is usually ignored, or made solely on the basis of conventions in one's field (i.e., the alpha level that defines statistical significance). The choice of stringent criteria (e.g., $\alpha = .01$) is sometimes interpreted as scientifically rigorous, whereas the choice of less rigorous criteria (e.g., $\alpha = .10$) is sometimes derided as "soft science." Nothing could be farther from the truth. In fact, any decision about alpha levels implies some wish to balance Type I and Type II errors, and power analysis is absolutely necessary if any kind of sense is to be made out of that balance. Once researchers appreciate the implications of choosing different alpha levels for the statistical power of their studies, they are more likely to make sensible choices about this critical parameter.

If power analysis is taken seriously, it is likely that fewer studies with small samples or insufficient sensitivity will be done. Researchers benefit substantially by knowing whether the study they have in mind has any real likelihood of detecting treatment effects. And the indirect benefits to the field as a whole that might come with a decline in small sample research are even greater than the benefits to the individual researcher.

Interpreting Research.   One criticism of tests of the traditional null hypothesis is that they routinely can mislead researchers and readers. Researchers who uncover a significant result are likely to confuse that with an important or meaningful result. This is hardly surprising; most dictionary definitions of significant include "importance," "weight," or "meaning" as synonyms. Similarly, nonsignificant is easily confused with "not important" or "nonmeaningful." As power analysis clearly shows, very meaningful and important treatment effects are likely to be nonsignificant if the study lacks power, whereas completely trivial effects are likely to be significant if enough data are collected. It is impossible to sensibly interpret significant or nonsignificant results without considering the level of statistical power in the study that produced those results.

To give a concrete illustration, consider a dozen studies, all of which reported a nonsignificant correlation between attitudes toward drug use and subsequent drug consumption. What does this mean? If the studies are all based on small samples, it is entirely possible that there is a real and meaningful correlation between attitudes and subsequent behavior (e.g., if $N = 30$ and $\alpha = .05$, power for detecting a correlation as large as .30 is only .50), and the studies simply did not have enough power to detect it. On the other hand, if all of the studies included very large samples (e.g., $N = 2,500$), it could probably be concluded that there is essentially no relation between present attitudes and future behavior. Although the traditional null hypothesis might not be literally true in this instance, it would have to be very nearly true. With this much power, the studies reviewed would have almost certainly detected any consistent relation between attitudes and behavior.

Indirect Benefits of Power Analysis

The widespread use of power analysis is likely to confer many indirect benefits. Most notably, studies designed with statistical power in mind are likely to use large samples and sensitive procedures. Perhaps even more important, power analysis directs the researcher's attention toward the most important parameter of all: the effect size. The ultimate benefit of statistical power analysis may be that it forces researchers to think about the strength of the effects they study, rather than thinking only about whether or not a particular effect is significant.

Large Samples, Sensitive Procedures.   Small samples are the bane of social science research (J. E. Hunter & Schmidt, 1990; Schmidt, 1996). These studies produce unstable results, which in turn produce attempts to develop theories to "explain" what may be little more than sampling error. If power analyses were routinely included in the process of designing and planning studies, large samples would be the norm and sampling error would not loom so large as a barrier to cumulative progress in research.

Proponents of metanalysis (e.g., Schmidt, 1996) note that by combining the outcomes of multiple small sample studies, it is possible to draw sensible conclusions about effect sizes, even if the individual study samples are too small to provide either sufficient power or stable results. There is merit to this position, but there are also two problems with this solution to the problem of small samples. First, it creates a two-tiered structure in which the primary researchers do all the work with little possibility of rewards (i.e., they do studies that cannot be published because of insufficient power and sensitivity) and the metanalyst gets all the credit for amassing this material into an interpretable whole. Second, it leaves the metanalyst at the mercy of a pool of primary researchers. Unless there are many studies examining exactly the question the metanalyst wants to answer, the only alternatives are to change the question or to aggregate together studies that in fact differ in important ways. Neither alternative seems attractive, and if power analysis becomes routine, neither will be strictly necessary. If future studies include large samples and sensitive procedures, the need for metanalyses will become less pressing than it is today.

The decision to use large samples is itself likely to improve other aspects of the research. For example, if it is known that considerable time and resources will need to be devoted to data collection, it will probably take more care to pretest, use reliable measures, follow well-laid-out procedures, and so on. In contrast, if running a study amounts to little more than rounding up 25 undergraduates and herding them to the lab, the need for careful planning, precise measurement, and so on may not be pressing. In large sample research, there may only be one chance to get things right, and there is less of a chance one will rely on shoddy measures, incomplete procedures, and so forth. The net result of all this is that studies carried out with careful attention to statistical power are likely to be better and more useful than studies carried without any regard for power.

Focus on Effect Size.   A scan of most social science journals shows that the outcomes of significance tests are routinely reported, but effect size information is often nowhere to be found. Statistical training tends to focus attention on p values and significance levels, and not on the substantive question of how well treatments, interventions, tests, and so on, work (See Cowles, 1989, for an historical analysis of why social scientists focus on significance tests). One of the most important advantages of statistical power analysis is that it makes it virtually impossible to ignore effect sizes.

The whole point of statistical analysis is to help researchers understand their data, and it has become increasingly clear over the years that an exclusive focus on significance testing is an impediment to understanding what the data mean (J. Cohen, 1994; Schmidt, 1996). Statistical power analysis forces them to think about the sort of effect to be expected, or at least about the sort of effect researchers want to be able to detect. And, once they start thinking along these lines, it is unlikely they will forget to think about the sort of effect actually found. If power analysis did nothing more than direct researchers' attention to the size of their effects, it would be well worth the effort.

Costs Associated With Power Analysis

Statistical power analysis brings a number of benefits, but there are also costs. Most notably, researchers who pay attention to statistical power will find it harder to carry out studies than researchers who do not think about power when planning or evaluating studies. Most researchers have done studies with small samples and insufficient power and have "gotten away with it", in the sense that they reported significant results. Even when power is low, there is always some chance that H_0 will be rejected, and a clever researcher can make a career out of "getting lucky." Power analysis will lead to fewer small sample studies, which in the long run might mean fewer studies period. It is relatively easy to do a dozen small sample studies with the knowledge that some will and some will not work. It is not so easy to do a dozen large sample studies, and one long-term result of applying power analysis is that the sheer number of studies performed in a field might go down. This is not necessarily a bad thing, at least if many low quality, small sample studies are replaced with a few higher quality, large sample studies. Nevertheless, the prospects for building a lengthy vita by doing dozens of studies might be diminished if serious attention is paid to power analysis.

The most serious cost that might be associated with the widespread use of power analysis is an overemphasis on scientific conservatism. If studies are hard to carry out, and require significant resources (time, money, energy), there may be less willingness to try new ideas and approaches or to test creative hypotheses. The long-term prospects for scientific progress are not good if researchers are unwilling or unable to take risks or try new ideas.

Implications of Power Analysis: Can Power Be too High?

Throughout, this book has advocated paying attention to the probability that researchers will be able to reject a null hypothesis they believe to be wrong (i.e., power). The pitfalls of low power are reasonably obvious, but it is worth considering whether power can be too high. Suppose the advice laid out in this book is followed, and a study is designed with a very high level of power (e.g., $p = .95$). One implication is that there is little real doubt about the outcomes of these statistical tests; with few exceptions, these tests will yield significant outcomes.

When power is extreme (either high or low), researchers are not likely to learn much by conducting a formal hypothesis test. This might imply that power can be too high. But, even when the outcome of a formal statistical hypothesis test is virtually known in advance, statistical analysis still has clear and obvious value. First, the statistics used in hypothesis testing usually provide an effect size estimate, or the information needed to make this estimate. Even if the statistical test itself provided little new information (with very high or very low power, it is known how things will turn out), the process of carrying out a statistical test usually provides information that can be used to evaluate the stability and potential replicability of the results.

Consider, for example, the familiar t test. The t statistic is a ratio of the difference between sample means to the standard error of the difference.[1] If the level of power in the study is very high, tests of the significance of t might not be all that informative; high power means it will exceed the threshold for significance in virtually all cases. However, the value of the t is still informative, because it gives you an easy way of determining the standard error term, which in turn can be used in forming confidence intervals. For example, if the M1 - M2 = 10.0 and t = 2.50, then it follows that the standard error of the difference between the means is 4.0 (i.e., 10.0/2.5), and a 95% confidence interval for the difference between means would be 7.84 units wide (i.e., 1.96 x 4.0). This confidence interval gives a very concrete indication of how much variation one might be expected from study to study when comparing M1 to M2.

In general, the standard error terms for test statistics tend to become smaller as samples get larger. This is a concrete illustration of the general principle that large samples provide stable and consistent statistical estimates, whereas small samples provide unstable estimates. Even in settings where the significance of a particular statistical test is not in doubt, confidence intervals provide very useful information. Obtaining a confidence interval allows researchers to determine just how much sampling error might be expected in the statistical estimates.

The previous paragraph illustrates a distinction that is sometimes blurred by researchers (i.e., the distinction between statistical analysis and null hypothesis testing). Researchers in the behavioral and social sciences have tended to overemphasize formal hypothesis tests, and have paid too little attention to critical questions such as "how large is the effect of the treatments studied here?" (J. Cohen, 1994; Cowles, 1989). Ironically, serious attention to the topic of power analysis is likely to reduce researchers' dependence on significance testing. The more that is known about power, the more likely that steps are to be taken to maximize statistical power, which means that rejecting the null should be nearly a foregone conclusion. Once it is understood that the null hypothesis test is not the most important facet of the statistical analysis, researchers are likely to turn their attention to the aspects of the analysis that are more important, such as estimating effect sizes.

---

[1] i.e., $t = \dfrac{M_1 - M_2}{\text{Standard error of the difference between means}}$ or $t = \dfrac{M_1 - M_2}{\sqrt{\dfrac{\sigma_1^2}{n_1} + \dfrac{\sigma_2^2}{n_2}}}$

Does all this mean that null hypothesis tests should be abandoned? The answer is probably not. First, as has been noted throughout this book, many of the outstanding criticisms of the null hypothesis can be easily addressed by shifting from tests of point hypotheses (e.g., that treatments have no effect whatsoever) to tests of range or interval hypothesis (e.g., that the effects of treatments fall within some range of values denoting small effects). Second, judging from the historical record, the prospects for fundamental changes in research strategies seem poor (Cowles, 1989). Statisticians have been arguing for decades that the use of confidence intervals is preferable to the use of null hypothesis tests, with little apparent effect on actual research practice. Critics of null hypothesis tests have not suggested an alternative that is both viable and likely to be widely adopted. There is every indication that null hypothesis tests are here to stay, and careful attention should be given to methods of making the process of hypothesis testing as useful and informative as possible. Careful attention to the principles of power analysis is likely to lead to better research and better statistical analyses.

CONCLUSIONS

Power analysis has profound implications for statistical hypothesis testing, regardless of whether the traditional null hypothesis (i.e., that treatments had no effect whatsoever) or a minimum-effect null hypothesis (e.g., that the effects of treatments are at best) is tested. In tests of the traditional null, Type I errors are very unlikely (because the traditional null is essentially false by definition), and the only real concern in structuring significance tests should be for maximizing power. This can be done by collecting huge samples, or by using extremely sensitive procedures, but there is an easier way to accomplish this goal. When testing the traditional null hypothesis, always set the alpha level as high as you dare. Unfortunately, the weight of tradition rarely allows researchers to choose an alpha level higher than .05 (alpha of .10 is seen in some social science research, but even there, it is barely tolerated). Never choose a more stringent level, unless there is some very unusual and compelling reason to do so.

Tests of minimum-effect null hypotheses are less familiar, but in fact, virtually everything that is known about hypothesis testing applies to tests of this sort. In fact, much of what is already known about hypothesis testing applies better to tests of minimum-effect null hypotheses than to tests of the traditional null.

When testing minimum-effect null hypotheses, seriously consider the possibility that the null hypothesis will be true. This opens the door for what is sometimes considered statistical heresy (i.e., accepting the null). It also opens the door to the possibility that Type I errors will be made, which means that alpha levels, statistical tests, balancing Type I and Type II errors, and so on have some real meaning in this context.

Power analysis has many benefits. It helps researchers make informed decisions about the design of their own research (especially about the number of cases needed and the choice of alpha levels), and it also helps make sense out of other researchers' significant or nonsignificant results. However, the indirect benefits of power analysis may be the most important. Power analysis is likely to lead to the use of larger samples, which in turn will often encourage the use of better measures, more pretests, more carefully designed procedures, and so on. Power analysis also helps to focus attention on effect sizes, rather than focusing exclusively on the p value associated with some statistical test. All of this is likely to improve the quality and consistency of social science research.

There are some costs associated with using power analysis. In particular, it is often hard to obtain samples large enough to provide sufficient power. This is especially true in studies where the central hypothesis involves some complex higher order interaction between multiple independent variables. It can be prohibitively difficult to obtain enough power to sensibly test such hypotheses. Reliance on power analysis may also indirectly discourage researchers form trying out new concepts, hypotheses, or procedures.

Throughout, this book has advocated careful attention to statistical power. As the level of power increases, there should be less and less doubt about the outcomes of null hypothesis tests. Ironically, careful attention to power is likely to decrease the relative importance of null hypothesis tests, and increase the attention paid to other aspects of statistical analysis, notably effect sizes, and confidence intervals. This is a good thing. Null hypothesis testing is valuable (especially when testing minimum-effect null hypotheses), but it should not be the primary focus of statistical analysis. Rather, well-conducted null hypothesis tests should be only a part of the analytic arsenal bought to bear when attempting to determine what the data really mean. Power analysis is the first step in carrying out sensible tests of both traditional and minimum-effect null hypotheses.

Appendix A

WORKING WITH THE NONCENTRAL
F DISTRIBUTION

The noncentral F distribution is hard to tabulate because it depends on three separate parameters (v1, v2 and, λ), but there is a reasonably simple approximation based on the central F distribution (Horton, 1978; Patnaik, 1949; see also Tiku & Yip, 1978). The noncentral F [F(v1, v2, λ)] is distributed approximately as the central F [$F^*(g, v2)$], with:

$$g = (v1 + \lambda)^2 / (v1 + 2\lambda) \qquad (A1)$$

and

$$F^*(g, v2) = F(v1, v2, p1) / [(v1 + \lambda)/ v1] \qquad (A2)$$

where F(v1, v2, p1) is the central F value that has a probability value of p1. Equation A2 estimates the central F that approximates any specific noncentral F value.

For example, suppose that in a study where 123 subjects are randomly assigned to one of three treatments, it is found that $SS_{treatments} = 10$ and $MS_e = 2$ (which means that $R^2 = .04$, or treatments account for 4% of the variance in this study). The F statistic used to test the hypothesis that treatments have no effect would have degrees of freedom of v1 = 2 and v2 = 120, and the value of F would be 2.50 [i.e, $MS_{treatments} = 10/v1 = 10/2 = 5$; F (2, 120) = 5/2 = 2.50]. The sum of squares for treatments and the mean square error give enough information to estimate the noncentrality parameter ($\lambda = 10/2 = 5.0$), and this in turn allows an estimate of the noncentral F distribution for the study.

Suppose researchers want to test the traditional null hypothesis of no treatment effect. The critical value of F for testing the traditional null with degrees of freedom of 2 and 120 and $\alpha = .05$ is 3.07. Using Equations A1 and A2, it is found that $g = 4.08$ and $F^*(4, 120) = .877$. At 4 and 120 degrees of freedom, approximately 50% of the central F distribution lies above a value of .877. Thus, the power of this statistical test is about .50, given the effect found in the study.

Another alternative is to use a computer program specifically designed for computing probabilities in the noncentral F distribution. For example, it is possible to obtain estimates of the appropriate noncentral F using simple functions that are built into a number of widely used programs (e.g., SPSS, Excel). In SPSS, the statement

COMPUTE p = NCDF.F ($F_{observed}$, v1, v2, v2 $*PV/(1 - PV)$)

calculates the percentage of the noncentral F distribution that is below the value of the observed F [where $\lambda = v2 *PV/(1-PV)$]. So, if researchers wanted to test the hypothesis that treatments accounted for 1% or less of the variance in outcomes, all they would need to do would be to insert the F obtained in the study into the COMPUTE statement (using $PV = .01$ to reflect the minimum effect of interest). Researchers can reject the hypothesis (with $\alpha = .05$) that the treatments account for 1% or less of the variance if the value obtained from this COMPUTE statement is .95 or greater.

Approximations like those listed earlier work reasonably well, but to achieve a high degree of accuracy, it is best to compute the cumulative density function of the F distribution, which is given by:

$$p(F \leq F^*) = \int_0^{F^*} p(F)dF = 1 - e^{\frac{-\lambda}{2}} \sum_{r=0}^{\infty} \frac{\left(\frac{\lambda}{2}\right)^r}{r!} I_{u_0}\left(\frac{v2}{2}, \frac{v1}{2} + r\right) \qquad \text{(A3)}$$

where:

$$u_0 = \frac{1}{\left(1 + \frac{v1}{v2}F^*\right)} \qquad \text{(A4)}$$

F^* is the critical value of the desired distribution, l is the noncentrality parameter, v1 and v2 are the degrees of freedom in the numerator and denominator respectively, and $I_U(a, b)$ is the incomplete beta function. For example, the traditional null hypothesis critical value level for an F test with v1 = 2, v2 = 30, and $\alpha = .05$ can be obtained by setting Equation A3 to .95 and solving it for F^* with $\lambda = 0$ (i.e., the central F distribution). In this case, F^* equals 3.32, which is the value found in the back of any statistics text. This cumulative density function was used to generate the One-Stop F Table shown in Appendix B.

Appendix B

ONE-STOP *F* TABLE

One Stop F Table

v2	Hyp	F for	1	2	3	4	5	6	7	8	v1 9	10	12	15	20	30	40	60	120
3	nil	α=.05	10.13	9.55	9.28	9.12	9.01	8.94	8.89	8.85	8.81	8.79	8.74	8.70	8.66	8.62	8.59	8.57	8.55
	nil	α=.01	34.12	30.82	29.46	28.71	28.24	27.91	27.67	27.49	27.35	27.23	27.05	26.87	26.69	26.50	26.41	26.32	26.22
		pow .5	8.26	7.21	6.78	6.54	6.39	6.29	6.22	6.16	6.12	6.08	6.02	5.97	5.91	5.86	5.82	5.80	5.76
		pow .8	18.17	15.70	14.83	14.42	14.19	13.93	13.85	13.69	13.66	13.64	13.55	13.48	13.42	13.30	13.26	13.17	12.66
	1%	α=.05	10.43	9.70	9.37	9.19	9.07	8.99	8.93	8.88	8.84	8.81	8.77	8.72	8.67	8.63	8.60	8.58	8.55
	1%	α=.01	35.15	31.28	29.75	28.93	28.41	28.05	27.79	27.59	27.44	27.31	27.12	26.93	26.73	26.53	26.43	26.33	26.23
		pow .5	8.53	7.33	6.85	6.60	6.44	6.33	6.25	6.19	6.14	6.10	6.04	5.98	5.92	5.86	5.83	5.81	5.79
		pow .8	18.72	16.04	14.96	14.50	14.25	13.98	13.89	13.82	13.69	13.66	13.56	13.48	13.42	13.34	13.31	13.25	13.07
	5%	α=.05	11.72	10.30	9.76	9.48	9.30	9.18	9.09	9.02	8.97	8.92	8.86	8.79	8.73	8.66	8.63	8.59	8.56
	5%	α=.01	39.41	33.23	31.00	29.84	29.13	28.64	28.30	28.03	27.82	27.66	27.41	27.15	26.90	26.64	26.52	26.39	26.26
		pow .5	9.57	7.82	7.17	6.83	6.62	6.48	6.38	6.30	6.24	6.19	6.12	6.04	5.97	5.89	5.86	5.82	5.80
		pow .8	20.77	17.02	15.60	14.98	14.63	14.30	14.16	14.07	13.90	13.86	13.72	13.62	13.51	13.40	13.38	13.33	13.18
4	nil	α=.05	7.71	6.94	6.59	6.39	6.26	6.16	6.09	6.04	6.00	5.96	5.91	5.86	5.80	5.75	5.72	5.69	5.66
	nil	α=.01	21.20	18.00	16.69	15.98	15.52	15.21	14.98	14.80	14.66	14.55	14.37	14.20	14.02	13.84	13.75	13.65	13.56
		pow .5	6.68	5.48	5.00	4.73	4.55	4.43	4.34	4.27	4.22	4.17	4.10	4.03	3.96	3.89	3.86	3.82	3.78
		pow .8	14.17	11.30	10.22	9.66	9.24	9.02	8.86	8.75	8.60	8.53	8.44	8.30	8.19	8.04	7.95	7.87	7.80
	1%	α=.05	8.02	7.08	6.68	6.45	6.31	6.20	6.13	6.07	6.03	5.99	5.93	5.87	5.81	5.75	5.72	5.69	5.66
	1%	α=.01	22.05	18.36	16.92	16.14	15.65	15.31	15.06	14.87	14.72	14.60	14.42	14.24	14.05	13.86	13.76	13.66	13.56
		pow .5	6.94	5.60	5.07	4.78	4.60	4.46	4.37	4.30	4.24	4.19	4.12	4.05	3.97	3.90	3.86	3.82	3.79
		pow .8	14.64	11.50	10.34	9.75	9.39	9.07	8.91	8.78	8.69	8.56	8.46	8.32	8.20	8.05	7.96	7.88	7.88
	5%	α=.05	9.31	7.67	7.05	6.72	6.52	6.38	6.28	6.20	6.14	6.09	6.02	5.94	5.86	5.79	5.75	5.71	5.67
	5%	α=.01	25.49	19.86	17.85	16.81	16.17	15.74	15.42	15.19	15.00	14.85	14.63	14.40	14.17	13.93	13.82	13.70	13.58
		pow .5	8.05	6.10	5.39	5.01	4.77	4.61	4.50	4.40	4.33	4.28	4.19	4.10	4.02	3.93	3.88	3.84	3.80
		pow .8	16.63	12.42	10.93	10.18	9.65	9.36	9.15	9.00	8.82	8.73	8.61	8.43	8.25	8.12	8.00	7.91	7.78
5	nil	α=.05	6.61	5.79	5.41	5.19	5.05	4.95	4.88	4.82	4.77	4.73	4.68	4.62	4.56	4.50	4.46	4.43	4.40
	nil	α=.01	16.26	13.27	12.06	11.39	10.97	10.67	10.46	10.29	10.16	10.05	9.89	9.72	9.55	9.38	9.29	9.20	9.11
		pow .5	5.91	4.66	4.14	3.87	3.70	3.57	3.48	3.41	3.35	3.31	3.23	3.15	3.08	3.00	2.96	2.91	2.87
		pow .8	12.35	9.38	8.19	7.60	7.24	6.94	6.77	6.59	6.50	6.43	6.28	6.11	5.97	5.83	5.74	5.65	5.54
	1%	α=.05	6.94	5.93	5.50	5.26	5.10	4.99	4.91	4.85	4.80	4.76	4.70	4.63	4.57	4.50	4.47	4.44	4.40
	1%	α=.01	17.07	13.61	12.26	11.54	11.08	10.76	10.53	10.35	10.21	10.10	9.93	9.75	9.58	9.39	9.30	9.21	9.12
		pow .5	6.20	4.78	4.24	3.93	3.75	3.61	3.51	3.44	3.37	3.33	3.25	3.17	3.09	3.00	2.96	2.92	2.88
		pow .8	12.85	9.59	8.38	7.68	7.30	6.99	6.81	6.68	6.53	6.46	6.30	6.17	5.98	5.84	5.76	5.66	5.54
	5%	α=.05	8.31	6.54	5.88	5.53	5.32	5.17	5.06	4.98	4.91	4.86	4.78	4.70	4.62	4.54	4.49	4.45	4.41
	5%	α=.01	20.28	14.97	13.10	12.13	11.54	11.14	10.85	10.63	10.45	10.31	10.10	9.89	9.68	9.46	9.35	9.24	9.13
		pow .5	7.42	5.33	4.56	4.18	3.94	3.77	3.65	3.55	3.48	3.42	3.32	3.23	3.13	3.03	2.98	2.93	2.88
		pow .8	14.92	10.51	8.90	8.11	7.64	7.27	7.05	6.84	6.72	6.62	6.44	6.24	6.07	5.89	5.78	5.67	5.55

Hyp - hypothesis being tested: nil = traditional null; 1% = treatments account for 1% or less of the variance;
5% = reatments account for 5% or less of the variance in outcomes

F for - F values provided for alpha levels of .05 and .01; for traditional null (nil) and minimum-effect (1% and 5%) null hypotheses.

One Stop F Table

	Hyp																			
6	nil	α=.05	5.99	5.14	4.76	4.53	4.39	4.28	4.21	4.15	4.10	4.06	4.00	3.94	3.87	3.81	3.77	3.74	3.70
	nil	α=.01	13.74	10.92	9.78	9.15	8.75	8.47	8.26	8.10	7.98	7.87	7.72	7.56	7.40	7.23	7.14	7.06	6.97
		pow.5	5.45	4.15	3.67	3.39	3.21	3.08	2.99	2.92	2.86	2.82	2.74	2.66	2.58	2.49	2.45	2.40	2.36
		pow.8	11.33	8.29	7.15	6.51	6.12	5.84	5.65	5.50	5.38	5.28	5.10	4.95	4.80	4.65	4.56	4.46	4.36
	1%	α=.05	6.35	5.30	4.85	4.60	4.44	4.33	4.24	4.18	4.13	4.08	4.02	3.95	3.89	3.82	3.78	3.74	3.71
	1%	α=.01	14.56	11.25	9.98	9.29	8.85	8.55	8.33	8.16	8.03	7.92	7.76	7.59	7.42	7.24	7.15	7.06	6.97
		pow.5	5.77	4.32	3.75	3.45	3.25	3.12	3.02	2.95	2.89	2.84	2.76	2.68	2.59	2.50	2.45	2.41	2.36
		pow.8	11.86	8.54	7.28	6.60	6.19	5.90	5.69	5.53	5.41	5.31	5.16	5.00	4.82	4.66	4.56	4.46	4.35
	5%	α=.05	7.82	5.94	5.25	4.89	4.66	4.51	4.40	4.31	4.24	4.19	4.11	4.02	3.94	3.85	3.80	3.76	3.71
	5%	α=.01	17.73	12.58	10.78	9.86	9.29	8.91	8.63	8.42	8.25	8.12	7.92	7.72	7.51	7.30	7.20	7.09	6.99
		pow.5	7.11	4.88	4.13	3.72	3.47	3.29	3.17	3.06	2.98	2.93	2.83	2.74	2.64	2.53	2.48	2.42	2.37
		pow.8	14.05	9.45	7.88	7.04	6.53	6.18	5.93	5.70	5.55	5.43	5.26	5.08	4.90	4.69	4.60	4.49	4.36
7	nil	α=.05	5.59	4.74	4.35	4.12	3.97	3.87	3.79	3.73	3.68	3.64	3.57	3.51	3.44	3.38	3.34	3.30	3.27
	nil	α=.01	12.25	9.55	8.45	7.85	7.46	7.19	6.99	6.84	6.72	6.62	6.47	6.31	6.16	5.99	5.91	5.82	5.74
		pow.5	5.16	3.86	3.32	3.05	2.88	2.74	2.66	2.60	2.53	2.49	2.42	2.34	2.26	2.18	2.13	2.08	2.03
		pow.8	10.68	7.64	6.43	5.80	5.41	5.11	4.92	4.78	4.64	4.55	4.39	4.25	4.09	3.92	3.82	3.73	3.62
	1%	α=.05	5.98	4.90	4.45	4.19	4.03	3.91	3.82	3.76	3.71	3.66	3.60	3.53	3.46	3.38	3.35	3.31	3.27
	1%	α=.01	13.09	9.88	8.65	7.98	7.57	7.28	7.06	6.90	6.77	6.67	6.51	6.34	6.18	6.01	5.92	5.83	5.74
		pow.5	5.52	4.01	3.44	3.11	2.93	2.80	2.69	2.62	2.55	2.51	2.43	2.36	2.27	2.18	2.13	2.08	2.03
		pow.8	11.26	7.87	6.61	5.90	5.49	5.21	4.97	4.82	4.67	4.58	4.42	4.26	4.10	3.93	3.84	3.73	3.62
	5%	α=.05	7.56	5.59	4.87	4.49	4.26	4.10	3.99	3.90	3.83	3.77	3.68	3.60	3.51	3.42	3.37	3.32	3.28
	5%	α=.01	16.29	11.21	9.46	8.55	8.00	7.63	7.36	7.15	6.99	6.86	6.67	6.47	6.27	6.07	5.96	5.85	5.75
		pow.5	6.98	4.66	3.81	3.40	3.16	2.96	2.85	2.76	2.67	2.62	2.52	2.43	2.32	2.21	2.16	2.10	2.04
		pow.8	13.59	8.87	7.19	6.34	5.84	5.45	5.21	5.03	4.86	4.75	4.56	4.37	4.18	3.96	3.86	3.76	3.62
8	nil	α=.05	5.32	4.46	4.07	3.84	3.69	3.58	3.50	3.44	3.39	3.35	3.28	3.22	3.15	3.08	3.04	3.00	2.97
	nil	α=.01	11.26	8.65	7.59	7.01	6.63	6.37	6.18	6.03	5.91	5.81	5.67	5.52	5.36	5.20	5.12	5.03	4.95
		pow.5	4.94	3.63	3.12	2.82	2.66	2.52	2.41	2.36	2.30	2.24	2.18	2.11	2.04	1.95	1.91	1.86	1.80
		pow.8	10.22	7.17	5.99	5.33	4.95	4.65	4.44	4.30	4.16	4.05	3.91	3.75	3.59	3.41	3.33	3.23	3.12
	1%	α=.05	5.74	4.64	4.18	3.92	3.75	3.63	3.54	3.47	3.42	3.37	3.31	3.24	3.16	3.09	3.05	3.01	2.97
	1%	α=.01	12.14	8.99	7.79	7.15	6.74	6.46	6.25	6.09	5.96	5.86	5.70	5.54	5.38	5.21	5.13	5.04	4.95
		pow.5	5.36	3.79	3.22	2.88	2.71	2.56	2.45	2.39	2.32	2.29	2.20	2.13	2.05	1.96	1.91	1.86	1.80
		pow.8	10.86	7.42	6.14	5.44	5.03	4.72	4.49	4.34	4.20	4.12	3.93	3.77	3.60	3.42	3.34	3.23	3.12
	5%	α=.05	7.44	5.37	4.62	4.24	3.99	3.83	3.71	3.62	3.55	3.49	3.40	3.31	3.22	3.12	3.07	3.03	2.98
	5%	α=.01	15.41	10.35	8.61	7.72	7.18	6.81	6.54	6.34	6.19	6.06	5.86	5.67	5.47	5.27	5.17	5.07	4.96
		pow.5	6.94	4.48	3.65	3.20	2.92	2.76	2.62	2.54	2.45	2.38	2.30	2.20	2.10	2.00	1.94	1.88	1.81
		pow.8	13.34	8.47	6.79	5.90	5.35	5.01	4.74	4.56	4.39	4.25	4.07	3.88	3.69	3.48	3.37	3.26	3.14

Hyp - hypothesis being tested: nil = traditional null; 1% = treatments account for 1% or less of the variance; 5% = treatments account for 5% or less of the variance in outcomes

F for - F values provided for alpha levels of .05 and .01; for traditional null (nil) and minimum-effect (1% and 5%) null hypotheses. F-equivalent values needed for power of .50 and power of .80 (with α=.05) to reject that hypothesis are also provided

One Stop F Table

9	nil α=.05	5.11	4.26	3.86	3.63	3.48	3.37	3.29	3.23	3.18	3.14	3.07	3.01	2.94	2.86	2.83	2.79	2.75
	nil α=.01	10.56	8.02	6.99	6.42	6.06	5.80	5.61	5.47	5.35	5.26	5.11	4.96	4.81	4.65	4.57	4.48	4.40
	pow .5	4.80	3.48	2.94	2.64	2.48	2.35	2.25	2.17	2.11	2.09	2.01	1.95	1.86	1.79	1.75	1.70	1.64
	pow .8	9.90	6.84	5.64	4.99	4.60	4.31	4.10	3.94	3.80	3.73	3.56	3.41	3.22	3.06	2.97	2.87	2.76
	1% α=.05	5.58	4.45	3.98	3.72	3.54	3.42	3.34	3.27	3.21	3.17	3.10	3.02	2.95	2.87	2.83	2.79	2.75
	1% α=.01	11.49	8.38	7.20	6.57	6.17	5.89	5.69	5.53	5.41	5.30	5.15	4.99	4.83	4.66	4.58	4.49	4.40
	pow .5	5.22	3.66	3.04	2.75	2.54	2.39	2.28	2.20	2.17	2.11	2.03	1.96	1.89	1.80	1.75	1.70	1.64
	pow .8	10.57	7.11	5.80	5.13	4.69	4.38	4.15	3.98	3.87	3.76	3.43	3.43	3.01	2.91	2.98	2.81	2.76
	5% α=.05	7.39	5.23	4.46	4.06	3.81	3.64	3.51	3.42	3.34	3.28	3.19	3.10	3.01	2.91	2.86	2.81	2.76
	5% α=.01	14.85	9.78	8.04	7.16	6.62	6.25	5.99	5.79	5.63	5.50	5.31	5.12	4.92	4.72	4.62	4.52	4.42
	pow .5	6.96	4.39	3.50	3.04	2.80	2.60	2.46	2.36	2.27	2.24	2.13	2.02	1.93	1.84	1.78	1.72	1.65
	pow .8	13.22	8.22	6.48	5.58	5.06	4.68	4.41	4.20	4.04	3.94	3.73	3.52	3.32	3.12	3.01	2.89	2.77
10	nil α=.05	4.96	4.10	3.71	3.48	3.33	3.22	3.14	3.07	3.02	2.98	2.91	2.84	2.77	2.70	2.66	2.62	2.58
	nil α=.01	10.04	7.56	6.55	5.99	5.64	5.39	5.20	5.06	4.94	4.85	4.71	4.56	4.41	4.25	4.17	4.08	4.00
	pow .5	4.68	3.33	2.83	2.53	2.34	2.21	2.11	2.04	1.98	1.93	1.86	1.81	1.74	1.66	1.62	1.58	1.52
	pow .8	9.65	6.58	5.40	4.75	4.34	4.05	3.84	3.68	3.55	3.44	3.28	3.14	2.97	2.78	2.69	2.59	2.48
	1% α=.05	5.46	4.31	3.83	3.57	3.39	3.27	3.18	3.11	3.05	3.01	2.94	2.86	2.79	2.71	2.67	2.63	2.58
	1% α=.01	11.02	7.93	6.77	6.14	5.75	5.48	5.28	5.12	5.00	4.90	4.75	4.59	4.43	4.26	4.18	4.09	4.00
	pow .5	5.14	3.56	2.94	2.60	2.40	2.25	2.15	2.07	2.01	1.99	1.91	1.83	1.75	1.67	1.63	1.58	1.52
	pow .8	10.37	6.89	5.57	4.87	4.42	4.12	3.90	3.73	3.59	3.51	3.34	3.16	2.98	2.79	2.71	2.60	2.49
	5% α=.05	7.39	5.13	4.34	3.93	3.67	3.50	3.37	3.27	3.20	3.13	3.04	2.94	2.85	2.75	2.70	2.64	2.59
	5% α=.01	14.48	9.38	7.64	6.75	6.21	5.85	5.58	5.38	5.23	5.10	4.91	4.72	4.52	4.32	4.22	4.12	4.01
	pow .5	6.94	4.35	3.43	2.96	2.67	2.48	2.34	2.23	2.15	2.09	1.99	1.89	1.81	1.71	1.65	1.60	1.53
	pow .8	13.14	8.06	6.28	5.37	4.81	4.44	4.16	3.95	3.79	3.66	3.46	3.26	3.07	2.85	2.74	2.63	2.50
11	nil α=.05	4.84	3.98	3.59	3.36	3.20	3.09	3.01	2.95	2.90	2.85	2.79	2.72	2.65	2.57	2.53	2.49	2.45
	nil α=.01	9.65	7.21	6.22	5.67	5.32	5.07	4.89	4.74	4.63	4.54	4.40	4.25	4.10	3.94	3.86	3.78	3.69
	pow .5	4.59	3.24	2.70	2.40	2.21	2.09	1.99	1.92	1.87	1.82	1.76	1.69	1.63	1.55	1.51	1.48	1.43
	pow .8	9.45	6.38	5.19	4.54	4.12	3.84	3.63	3.47	3.34	3.24	3.08	2.92	2.76	2.57	2.47	2.38	2.27
	1% α=.05	5.37	4.20	3.72	3.45	3.27	3.15	3.06	2.99	2.93	2.88	2.81	2.74	2.66	2.58	2.54	2.49	2.45
	1% α=.01	10.67	7.60	6.44	5.82	5.43	5.16	4.96	4.81	4.69	4.59	4.44	4.28	4.12	3.96	3.87	3.78	3.69
	pow .5	5.09	3.44	2.86	2.53	2.32	2.17	2.07	1.99	1.93	1.88	1.78	1.71	1.64	1.56	1.52	1.48	1.43
	pow .8	10.22	6.69	5.39	4.68	4.24	3.94	3.72	3.55	3.41	3.30	3.11	2.94	2.77	2.58	2.48	2.39	2.27
	5% α=.05	7.42	5.08	4.26	3.83	3.57	3.39	3.26	3.16	3.08	3.02	2.92	2.82	2.72	2.62	2.57	2.51	2.46
	5% α=.01	14.23	9.09	7.34	6.45	5.91	5.55	5.28	5.08	4.93	4.80	4.61	4.41	4.22	4.02	3.92	3.81	3.71
	pow .5	7.00	4.27	3.38	2.90	2.61	2.41	2.23	2.13	2.05	1.98	1.89	1.80	1.71	1.60	1.55	1.50	1.44
	pow .8	13.14	7.91	6.14	5.22	4.65	4.27	3.96	3.76	3.59	3.46	3.26	3.06	2.86	2.64	2.53	2.41	2.28

Hyp - hypothesis being tested: nil = traditional null; 1% = treatments account for 1% or less of the variance;
    5% = treatments account for 5% or less of the variance in outcomes

F for - F values provided for alpha levels of .05 and .01; for traditional null (nil) and minimum-effect (1% and 5%) null hypotheses.
    F-equivalent values needed for power of .50 and power of .80 (with α=.05) to reject that hypothesis are also provided

One Stop F Table

12	nil	α=.05	4.74	3.89	3.49	3.26	3.11	3.00	2.91	2.85	2.80	2.75	2.69	2.62	2.54	2.47	2.43	2.38	2.34
	nil	α=.01	9.33	6.93	5.95	5.41	5.06	4.82	4.64	4.50	4.39	4.30	4.16	4.01	3.86	3.70	3.62	3.54	3.45
		pow .5	4.52	3.17	2.63	2.33	2.15	2.02	1.93	1.86	1.80	1.76	1.66	1.61	1.53	1.47	1.43	1.39	1.35
		pow .8	9.30	6.23	5.03	4.38	3.97	3.69	3.48	3.32	3.20	3.09	2.91	2.76	2.58	2.41	2.31	2.21	2.09
	1%	α=.05	5.31	4.12	3.63	3.36	3.18	3.06	2.96	2.89	2.83	2.79	2.71	2.64	2.56	2.48	2.43	2.39	2.34
	1%	α=.01	10.40	7.34	6.19	5.57	5.19	4.92	4.72	4.57	4.45	4.35	4.20	4.04	3.88	3.72	3.63	3.54	3.45
		pow .5	5.05	3.38	2.75	2.42	2.21	2.07	1.97	1.89	1.83	1.79	1.68	1.62	1.54	1.47	1.43	1.40	1.36
		pow .8	10.12	6.55	5.22	4.51	4.07	3.77	3.54	3.37	3.24	3.13	2.95	2.78	2.60	2.42	2.31	2.21	2.10
	5%	α=.05	7.47	5.04	4.20	3.76	3.49	3.31	3.17	3.07	2.99	2.93	2.83	2.73	2.62	2.52	2.46	2.41	2.35
	5%	α=.01	14.07	8.88	7.12	6.23	5.68	5.31	5.05	4.85	4.69	4.56	4.37	4.18	3.98	3.78	3.68	3.57	3.47
		pow .5	7.08	4.26	3.30	2.81	2.51	2.32	2.18	2.08	2.00	1.93	1.80	1.72	1.61	1.52	1.47	1.42	1.36
		pow .8	13.18	7.84	6.00	5.07	4.49	4.11	3.83	3.62	3.46	3.33	3.10	2.91	2.69	2.48	2.36	2.24	2.11
13	nil	α=.05	4.66	3.81	3.41	3.18	3.03	2.91	2.83	2.77	2.71	2.67	2.60	2.53	2.46	2.38	2.34	2.30	2.25
	nil	α=.01	9.07	6.70	5.74	5.21	4.86	4.62	4.44	4.30	4.19	4.10	3.96	3.82	3.66	3.51	3.43	3.34	3.25
		pow .5	4.46	3.11	2.57	2.27	2.09	1.97	1.83	1.77	1.71	1.67	1.62	1.53	1.46	1.39	1.34	1.32	1.29
		pow .8	9.17	6.10	4.91	4.26	3.85	3.57	3.33	3.17	3.05	2.95	2.80	2.62	2.45	2.27	2.16	2.06	1.95
	1%	α=.05	5.27	4.05	3.56	3.28	3.10	2.98	2.88	2.81	2.75	2.71	2.63	2.55	2.47	2.39	2.35	2.30	2.25
	1%	α=.01	10.20	7.13	5.99	5.37	4.99	4.72	4.52	4.37	4.25	4.15	4.00	3.85	3.69	3.52	3.44	3.35	3.26
		pow .5	5.02	3.34	2.70	2.36	2.16	2.02	1.92	1.80	1.74	1.70	1.64	1.55	1.47	1.40	1.36	1.32	1.29
		pow .8	10.03	6.44	5.11	4.40	3.95	3.65	3.43	3.23	3.10	2.99	2.83	2.64	2.46	2.28	2.18	2.07	1.96
	5%	α=.05	7.54	5.03	4.15	3.70	3.43	3.24	3.10	3.00	2.92	2.85	2.75	2.65	2.54	2.43	2.38	2.32	2.26
	5%	α=.01	13.98	8.73	6.95	6.05	5.50	5.13	4.86	4.66	4.50	4.38	4.18	3.99	3.79	3.59	3.48	3.38	3.27
		pow .5	7.16	4.26	3.27	2.78	2.48	2.28	2.14	1.99	1.91	1.85	1.76	1.64	1.54	1.45	1.38	1.35	1.30
		pow .8	13.24	7.79	5.92	4.97	4.39	4.01	3.73	3.49	3.32	3.19	2.99	2.77	2.56	2.34	2.21	2.10	1.97
14	nil	α=.05	4.60	3.74	3.34	3.11	2.96	2.85	2.76	2.70	2.65	2.60	2.53	2.46	2.39	2.31	2.27	2.22	2.18
	nil	α=.01	8.86	6.51	5.56	5.04	4.69	4.46	4.28	4.14	4.03	3.94	3.80	3.66	3.50	3.35	3.27	3.18	3.09
		pow .5	4.41	3.06	2.52	2.23	2.00	1.88	1.79	1.72	1.67	1.59	1.54	1.46	1.39	1.32	1.28	1.26	1.23
		pow .8	9.06	5.99	4.80	4.16	3.72	3.44	3.23	3.07	2.95	2.82	2.67	2.50	2.33	2.14	2.04	1.95	1.83
	1%	α=.05	5.24	4.00	3.50	3.22	3.04	2.91	2.82	2.75	2.69	2.64	2.56	2.49	2.40	2.32	2.27	2.23	2.18
	1%	α=.01	10.04	6.96	5.82	5.21	4.83	4.56	4.36	4.21	4.09	3.99	3.84	3.69	3.53	3.36	3.28	3.19	3.10
		pow .5	5.01	3.30	2.66	2.32	2.12	1.93	1.83	1.76	1.70	1.66	1.56	1.47	1.41	1.32	1.28	1.26	1.23
		pow .8	9.98	6.35	5.01	4.30	3.85	3.52	3.30	3.13	3.00	2.89	2.71	2.53	2.35	2.15	2.05	1.95	1.84
	5%	α=.05	7.62	5.02	4.13	3.66	3.38	3.19	3.05	2.94	2.86	2.79	2.69	2.58	2.47	2.36	2.31	2.25	2.19
	5%	α=.01	13.93	8.61	6.82	5.91	5.36	4.98	4.72	4.51	4.35	4.22	4.03	3.83	3.63	3.43	3.33	3.22	3.11
		pow .5	7.25	4.27	3.26	2.76	2.45	2.20	2.06	1.96	1.88	1.78	1.69	1.58	1.48	1.37	1.32	1.29	1.25
		pow .8	13.32	7.76	5.86	4.90	4.32	3.89	3.61	3.40	3.23	3.08	2.88	2.66	2.45	2.22	2.10	1.98	1.85

Hyp - hypothesis being tested: nil = traditional null; 1% = treatments account for 1% or less of the variance;
5% = treatments account for 5% or less of the variance in outcomes

F for - F values provided for alpha levels of .05 and .01; for traditional null (nil) and minimum-effect (1% and 5%) null hypotheses.
F-equivalent values needed for power of .50 and power of .80 (with α=.05) to reject that hypothesis are also provided

One Stop F Table

15 nil α=.05	4.54	3.68	3.29	3.06	2.90	2.79	2.71	2.64	2.59	2.54	2.47	2.40	2.33	2.25	2.20	2.16	2.11
nil α=.01	8.68	6.36	5.42	4.89	4.56	4.32	4.14	4.00	3.89	3.81	3.67	3.52	3.37	3.21	3.13	3.05	2.96
pow .5	4.37	3.02	2.48	2.14	1.96	1.84	1.75	1.64	1.59	1.56	1.47	1.39	1.34	1.27	1.22	1.20	1.17
pow .8	8.96	5.90	4.71	4.04	3.63	3.35	3.15	2.96	2.84	2.74	2.57	2.40	2.23	2.05	1.94	1.84	1.73
1% α=.05	5.22	3.96	3.45	3.17	2.99	2.86	2.76	2.69	2.63	2.58	2.51	2.43	2.34	2.26	2.21	2.16	2.12
1% α=.01	9.91	6.82	5.68	5.08	4.69	4.43	4.23	4.08	3.96	3.86	3.71	3.56	3.40	3.23	3.14	3.05	2.96
pow .5	5.00	3.27	2.63	2.29	2.03	1.89	1.80	1.73	1.63	1.59	1.53	1.44	1.35	1.27	1.24	1.20	1.18
pow .8	9.93	6.28	4.93	4.22	3.75	3.44	3.22	3.05	2.89	2.79	2.63	2.45	2.25	2.06	1.96	1.85	1.73
5% α=.05	7.71	5.03	4.11	3.63	3.34	3.15	3.01	2.90	2.81	2.74	2.64	2.53	2.42	2.31	2.25	2.19	2.13
5% α=.01	13.91	8.53	6.71	5.80	5.24	4.86	4.59	4.39	4.23	4.10	3.90	3.71	3.50	3.30	3.19	3.09	2.98
pow .5	7.35	4.29	3.26	2.74	2.38	2.18	2.04	1.93	1.81	1.75	1.62	1.51	1.43	1.33	1.26	1.23	1.19
pow .8	13.41	7.75	5.82	4.85	4.22	3.83	3.54	3.33	3.13	3.00	2.78	2.56	2.35	2.13	2.00	1.88	1.75
16 nil α=.05	4.49	3.63	3.24	3.01	2.85	2.74	2.66	2.59	2.54	2.49	2.42	2.35	2.27	2.19	2.15	2.10	2.06
nil α=.01	8.53	6.23	5.29	4.77	4.44	4.20	4.03	3.89	3.78	3.69	3.55	3.41	3.26	3.10	3.02	2.93	2.84
pow .5	4.33	2.98	2.39	2.10	1.92	1.80	1.67	1.61	1.56	1.53	1.44	1.36	1.28	1.22	1.18	1.15	1.12
pow .8	8.88	5.83	4.61	3.97	3.56	3.28	3.05	2.89	2.77	2.67	2.49	2.32	2.14	1.96	1.86	1.76	1.64
1% α=.05	5.20	3.92	3.41	3.13	2.94	2.81	2.72	2.64	2.58	2.53	2.46	2.38	2.29	2.20	2.16	2.11	2.06
1% α=.01	9.81	6.71	5.57	4.96	4.58	4.31	4.12	3.97	3.85	3.75	3.60	3.45	3.29	3.12	3.03	2.94	2.85
pow .5	5.00	3.25	2.60	2.26	2.00	1.86	1.77	1.65	1.60	1.56	1.46	1.38	1.29	1.23	1.18	1.15	1.13
pow .8	9.90	6.22	4.87	4.15	3.68	3.37	3.15	2.95	2.82	2.71	2.53	2.35	2.16	1.98	1.87	1.76	1.65
5% α=.05	7.81	5.04	4.10	3.61	3.32	3.12	2.97	2.86	2.77	2.70	2.59	2.48	2.37	2.25	2.19	2.13	2.07
5% α=.01	13.91	8.47	6.63	5.71	5.15	4.77	4.49	4.29	4.13	4.00	3.80	3.60	3.39	3.19	3.08	2.97	2.86
pow .5	7.45	4.31	3.26	2.73	2.36	2.16	2.02	1.86	1.79	1.73	1.60	1.49	1.37	1.28	1.22	1.18	1.14
pow .8	13.52	7.75	5.79	4.80	4.17	3.77	3.48	3.24	3.07	2.94	2.71	2.49	2.26	2.04	1.92	1.80	1.66
17 nil α=.05	4.45	3.59	3.20	2.96	2.81	2.70	2.61	2.55	2.49	2.45	2.38	2.31	2.23	2.15	2.10	2.06	2.01
nil α=.01	8.40	6.11	5.19	4.67	4.34	4.10	3.93	3.79	3.68	3.59	3.45	3.31	3.16	3.00	2.92	2.83	2.75
pow .5	4.24	2.95	2.36	2.07	1.89	1.78	1.64	1.58	1.54	1.46	1.37	1.30	1.23	1.15	1.14	1.09	1.08
pow .8	8.79	5.76	4.55	3.90	3.49	3.21	2.98	2.83	2.70	2.58	2.41	2.24	2.06	1.88	1.79	1.67	1.56
1% α=.05	5.20	3.89	3.38	3.09	2.91	2.77	2.68	2.60	2.54	2.49	2.41	2.33	2.25	2.16	2.11	2.06	2.01
1% α=.01	9.73	6.62	5.47	4.87	4.48	4.22	4.02	3.87	3.75	3.65	3.50	3.35	3.19	3.02	2.93	2.84	2.75
pow .5	5.00	3.23	2.58	2.18	1.98	1.84	1.69	1.62	1.57	1.49	1.44	1.36	1.27	1.18	1.14	1.11	1.08
pow .8	9.88	6.17	4.81	4.06	3.62	3.31	3.06	2.89	2.76	2.63	2.47	2.29	2.10	1.90	1.80	1.69	1.57
5% α=.05	7.91	5.06	4.09	3.60	3.29	3.09	2.94	2.83	2.74	2.67	2.56	2.44	2.33	2.21	2.15	2.09	2.02
5% α=.01	13.94	8.43	6.57	5.64	5.07	4.69	4.41	4.20	4.04	3.91	3.71	3.51	3.30	3.09	2.99	2.88	2.77
pow .5	7.55	4.34	3.26	2.73	2.35	2.15	1.95	1.85	1.77	1.66	1.58	1.43	1.36	1.24	1.19	1.14	1.09
pow .8	13.63	7.76	5.77	4.77	4.13	3.72	3.41	3.19	3.02	2.86	2.66	2.42	2.21	1.97	1.85	1.72	1.58

Hyp - hypothesis being tested: nil = traditional null; 1% = treatments account for 1% or less of the variance;
5% = reatments account for 5% or less of the variance in outcomes

F for - F values provided for alpha levels of .05 and .01; for traditional null (nil) and minimum-effect (1% and 5%) null hypotheses.

F-equivalent values needed for power of .50 and power of .80 (with α=.05) to reject that hypothesis are also provided

One Stop F Table

	Hyp																	
18	nil α=.05	4.41	3.55	3.16	2.93	2.77	2.66	2.58	2.51	2.46	2.41	2.34	2.27	2.19	2.11	2.06	2.02	1.97
	nil α=.01	8.28	6.01	5.09	4.58	4.25	4.01	3.84	3.71	3.60	3.51	3.37	3.23	3.08	2.92	2.84	2.75	2.66
	pow .5	4.21	2.87	2.34	2.05	1.87	1.70	1.62	1.55	1.47	1.44	1.35	1.28	1.21	1.13	1.08	1.06	1.04
	pow .8	8.73	5.68	4.49	3.84	3.44	3.13	2.93	2.77	2.62	2.52	2.35	2.19	2.01	1.82	1.71	1.61	1.50
1%	α=.05	5.19	3.87	3.35	3.06	2.87	2.74	2.64	2.57	2.50	2.45	2.38	2.30	2.21	2.12	2.07	2.02	1.97
1%	α=.01	9.67	6.54	5.39	4.78	4.40	4.13	3.94	3.79	3.67	3.57	3.42	3.27	3.11	2.94	2.85	2.76	2.66
	pow .5	5.01	3.21	2.56	2.16	1.95	1.82	1.67	1.60	1.55	1.47	1.38	1.30	1.22	1.14	1.11	1.06	1.04
	pow .8	9.87	6.13	4.76	4.01	3.56	3.26	3.01	2.84	2.71	2.58	2.39	2.22	2.03	1.84	1.73	1.62	1.50
5%	α=.05	8.02	5.09	4.09	3.59	3.28	3.07	2.92	2.80	2.71	2.64	2.52	2.41	2.29	2.17	2.11	2.05	1.98
5%	α=.01	13.99	8.40	6.52	5.58	5.00	4.62	4.34	4.13	3.97	3.83	3.63	3.43	3.22	3.01	2.90	2.79	2.68
	pow .5	7.65	4.37	3.27	2.66	2.34	2.14	1.94	1.83	1.76	1.65	1.52	1.42	1.31	1.20	1.13	1.09	1.06
	pow .8	13.75	7.77	5.76	4.71	4.10	3.69	3.37	3.14	2.98	2.81	2.59	2.37	2.14	1.91	1.77	1.65	1.52
19	nil α=.05	4.37	3.52	3.13	2.89	2.74	2.63	2.54	2.48	2.42	2.38	2.31	2.23	2.15	2.07	2.03	1.98	1.93
	nil α=.01	8.18	5.93	5.01	4.50	4.17	3.94	3.77	3.63	3.52	3.43	3.30	3.15	3.00	2.84	2.76	2.67	2.58
	pow .5	4.19	2.85	2.31	2.02	1.85	1.68	1.60	1.49	1.45	1.42	1.33	1.27	1.16	1.09	1.04	1.02	0.99
	pow .8	8.68	5.62	4.44	3.79	3.39	3.08	2.88	2.70	2.57	2.48	2.31	2.14	1.94	1.76	1.65	1.55	1.43
1%	α=.05	5.20	3.85	3.32	3.03	2.84	2.71	2.61	2.54	2.47	2.42	2.34	2.26	2.18	2.08	2.04	1.98	1.93
1%	α=.01	9.62	6.47	5.32	4.71	4.33	4.06	3.87	3.72	3.60	3.50	3.35	3.19	3.03	2.86	2.77	2.68	2.59
	pow .5	5.02	3.20	2.54	2.14	1.93	1.74	1.65	1.58	1.49	1.45	1.36	1.28	1.20	1.10	1.05	1.02	1.00
	pow .8	9.87	6.10	4.72	3.97	3.52	3.19	2.96	2.79	2.63	2.53	2.35	2.17	1.98	1.77	1.66	1.56	1.44
5%	α=.05	8.13	5.11	4.10	3.58	3.26	3.05	2.90	2.78	2.69	2.61	2.50	2.38	2.26	2.14	2.08	2.01	1.95
5%	α=.01	14.04	8.39	6.49	5.53	4.95	4.56	4.28	4.07	3.90	3.77	3.57	3.36	3.15	2.94	2.83	2.72	2.61
	pow .5	7.75	4.40	3.28	2.66	2.34	2.13	1.93	1.82	1.69	1.64	1.51	1.40	1.26	1.16	1.09	1.05	1.02
	pow .8	13.88	7.80	5.75	4.69	4.07	3.66	3.33	3.11	2.91	2.77	2.54	2.32	2.08	1.85	1.72	1.59	1.46
20	nil α=.05	4.34	3.49	3.10	2.87	2.71	2.60	2.51	2.45	2.39	2.35	2.28	2.20	2.12	2.04	1.99	1.95	1.90
	nil α=.01	8.09	5.85	4.94	4.43	4.10	3.87	3.70	3.56	3.46	3.37	3.23	3.09	2.94	2.78	2.69	2.61	2.52
	pow .5	4.17	2.82	2.29	2.00	1.77	1.66	1.58	1.47	1.43	1.35	1.32	1.21	1.14	1.05	1.01	0.99	0.97
	pow .8	8.63	5.58	4.39	3.75	3.32	3.04	2.83	2.65	2.53	2.45	2.26	2.07	1.90	1.70	1.60	1.50	1.38
1%	α=.05	5.20	3.84	3.30	3.01	2.82	2.69	2.59	2.51	2.45	2.39	2.32	2.23	2.14	2.05	2.00	1.95	1.90
1%	α=.01	9.58	6.41	5.26	4.65	4.27	4.00	3.80	3.65	3.53	3.44	3.29	3.13	2.97	2.80	2.71	2.62	2.52
	pow .5	5.03	3.19	2.47	2.13	1.92	1.73	1.63	1.57	1.47	1.43	1.34	1.23	1.15	1.06	1.04	0.99	0.97
	pow .8	9.87	6.07	4.66	3.93	3.48	3.14	2.92	2.75	2.59	2.49	2.31	2.11	1.92	1.72	1.62	1.51	1.39
5%	α=.05	8.20	5.15	4.11	3.58	3.26	3.04	2.88	2.76	2.67	2.59	2.47	2.36	2.23	2.11	2.05	1.98	1.91
5%	α=.01	14.11	8.38	6.46	5.49	4.91	4.51	4.23	4.02	3.85	3.71	3.51	3.30	3.09	2.88	2.77	2.65	2.54
	pow .5	7.95	4.43	3.30	2.67	2.34	2.12	1.92	1.81	1.68	1.63	1.50	1.35	1.24	1.12	1.06	1.02	0.98
	pow .8	14.02	7.82	5.75	4.68	4.05	3.63	3.30	3.08	2.88	2.74	2.51	2.27	2.04	1.79	1.66	1.54	1.40

Hyp - hypothesis being tested: nil = traditional null; 1% = treatments account for 1% or less of the variance;
5% = treatments account for 5% or less of the variance in outcomes

F for - F values provided for alpha levels of .05 and .01; for traditional null (nil) and minimum-effect (1% and 5%) null hypotheses.
F-equivalent values needed for power of .50 and power of .80 (with α=.05) to reject that hypothesis are also provided

One Stop F Table

	Hyp																			
21	nil	α=.05	4.32	3.47	3.07	2.84	2.68	2.57	2.49	2.42	2.37	2.32	2.25	2.17	2.09	2.01	1.96	1.92	1.86
	nil	α=.01	8.02	5.78	4.87	4.37	4.04	3.81	3.64	3.51	3.40	3.31	3.17	3.03	2.88	2.72	2.64	2.55	2.46
		pow .5	4.15	2.80	2.27	1.98	1.75	1.64	1.56	1.45	1.41	1.34	1.26	1.19	1.09	1.04	1.00	0.94	0.93
		pow .8	8.59	5.54	4.35	3.71	3.28	3.00	2.79	2.61	2.49	2.37	2.20	2.04	1.84	1.67	1.56	1.45	1.33
	1%	α=.05	5.21	3.83	3.29	2.99	2.80	2.66	2.56	2.48	2.42	2.37	2.29	2.21	2.12	2.02	1.97	1.92	1.87
	1%	α=.01	9.55	6.36	5.21	4.60	4.21	3.94	3.75	3.60	3.48	3.38	3.23	3.07	2.91	2.74	2.65	2.56	2.46
		pow .5	5.05	3.19	2.46	2.11	1.90	1.71	1.62	1.50	1.45	1.37	1.33	1.21	1.14	1.05	1.01	0.97	0.93
		pow .8	9.87	6.05	4.63	3.90	3.44	3.11	2.88	2.69	2.56	2.43	2.27	2.07	1.89	1.68	1.57	1.46	1.34
	5%	α=.05	8.30	5.18	4.12	3.58	3.25	3.03	2.87	2.74	2.65	2.57	2.45	2.33	2.21	2.08	2.02	1.95	1.88
	5%	α=.01	14.18	8.39	6.44	5.46	4.87	4.47	4.19	3.97	3.80	3.66	3.46	3.25	3.04	2.82	2.71	2.60	2.48
		pow .5	8.06	4.47	3.31	2.67	2.34	2.06	1.91	1.81	1.68	1.62	1.49	1.34	1.24	1.11	1.05	1.00	0.94
		pow .8	14.14	7.86	5.76	4.67	4.03	3.58	3.28	3.05	2.85	2.71	2.48	2.23	2.00	1.76	1.63	1.50	1.35
22	nil	α=.05	4.29	3.44	3.05	2.82	2.66	2.55	2.46	2.40	2.34	2.30	2.22	2.15	2.07	1.98	1.94	1.89	1.84
	nil	α=.01	7.94	5.72	4.82	4.31	3.99	3.76	3.59	3.45	3.35	3.26	3.12	2.98	2.83	2.67	2.58	2.49	2.40
		pow .5	4.13	2.79	2.25	1.97	1.74	1.62	1.49	1.44	1.35	1.32	1.24	1.18	1.08	1.00	0.97	0.92	0.90
		pow .8	8.55	5.50	4.32	3.67	3.24	2.96	2.73	2.58	2.43	2.33	2.16	2.00	1.81	1.62	1.52	1.40	1.29
	1%	α=.05	5.23	3.82	3.27	2.97	2.78	2.64	2.54	2.46	2.40	2.35	2.27	2.18	2.09	2.00	1.95	1.90	1.84
	1%	α=.01	9.53	6.32	5.16	4.55	4.16	3.90	3.70	3.55	3.43	3.33	3.18	3.02	2.86	2.69	2.60	2.50	2.41
		pow .5	5.06	3.18	2.45	2.10	1.89	1.70	1.61	1.49	1.44	1.36	1.27	1.20	1.09	1.01	0.97	0.94	0.90
		pow .8	9.88	6.03	4.60	3.87	3.41	3.08	2.85	2.66	2.52	2.39	2.21	2.04	1.83	1.63	1.53	1.42	1.29
	5%	α=.05	8.41	5.22	4.13	3.58	3.25	3.02	2.86	2.73	2.63	2.56	2.44	2.31	2.19	2.06	1.99	1.92	1.85
	5%	α=.01	14.26	8.40	6.43	5.44	4.84	4.44	4.15	3.93	3.76	3.62	3.41	3.20	2.99	2.77	2.66	2.54	2.43
		pow .5	8.17	4.51	3.33	2.68	2.34	2.06	1.91	1.75	1.67	1.56	1.43	1.33	1.19	1.07	1.02	0.95	0.92
		pow .8	14.27	7.89	5.77	4.66	4.02	3.56	3.26	3.00	2.82	2.66	2.43	2.20	1.95	1.71	1.58	1.45	1.31
23	nil	α=.05	4.27	3.42	3.03	2.80	2.64	2.53	2.44	2.37	2.32	2.27	2.20	2.13	2.05	1.96	1.91	1.86	1.81
	nil	α=.01	7.88	5.66	4.76	4.26	3.94	3.71	3.54	3.41	3.30	3.21	3.07	2.93	2.78	2.62	2.54	2.45	2.35
		pow .5	4.11	2.77	2.24	1.95	1.72	1.61	1.48	1.42	1.33	1.31	1.23	1.13	1.07	0.96	0.93	0.89	0.88
		pow .8	8.51	5.47	4.28	3.64	3.21	2.93	2.70	2.54	2.40	2.30	2.13	1.95	1.78	1.57	1.48	1.36	1.25
	1%	α=.05	5.24	3.81	3.26	2.96	2.76	2.62	2.52	2.44	2.38	2.33	2.24	2.16	2.07	1.97	1.92	1.87	1.82
	1%	α=.01	9.52	6.29	5.12	4.51	4.12	3.85	3.65	3.50	3.38	3.28	3.13	2.98	2.81	2.64	2.55	2.46	2.36
		pow .5	5.08	3.18	2.44	2.09	1.88	1.69	1.60	1.48	1.43	1.35	1.26	1.19	1.08	1.00	0.94	0.92	0.88
		pow .8	9.90	6.01	4.58	3.84	3.39	3.05	2.82	2.63	2.49	2.36	2.18	2.01	1.80	1.60	1.49	1.38	1.25
	5%	α=.05	8.52	5.26	4.15	3.59	3.25	3.02	2.85	2.72	2.62	2.54	2.42	2.30	2.17	2.04	1.97	1.90	1.83
	5%	α=.01	14.34	8.41	6.42	5.42	4.82	4.41	4.12	3.90	3.73	3.59	3.38	3.16	2.95	2.73	2.61	2.50	2.38
		pow .5	8.28	4.54	3.35	2.68	2.34	2.06	1.91	1.74	1.66	1.55	1.43	1.32	1.18	1.07	0.99	0.95	0.89
		pow .8	14.39	7.93	5.78	4.66	4.01	3.55	3.24	2.98	2.80	2.64	2.40	2.18	1.93	1.68	1.54	1.42	1.27

Hyp - hypothesis being tested: nil = traditional null; 1% = treatments account for 1% or less of the variance;
5% = reatments account for 5% or less of the variance in outcomes

F for - F values provided for alpha levels of .05 and .01; for traditional null (nil) and minimum-effect (1% and 5%) null hypotheses.
F-equivalent values needed for power of .50 and power of .80 (with α=.05) to reject that hypothesis are also provided

One Stop F Table

	Hyp																	
24	nil α=.05	4.25	3.40	3.01	2.78	2.62	2.51	2.42	2.35	2.30	2.25	2.18	2.11	2.03	1.94	1.89	1.84	1.79
	nil α=.01	7.82	5.61	4.72	4.22	3.90	3.67	3.50	3.36	3.26	3.17	3.03	2.89	2.74	2.58	2.49	2.40	2.31
	pow .5	4.10	2.76	2.22	1.94	1.71	1.60	1.47	1.41	1.32	1.30	1.22	1.12	1.02	0.96	0.90	0.87	0.85
	pow .8	8.48	5.44	4.25	3.61	3.18	2.90	2.67	2.52	2.37	2.27	2.10	1.92	1.73	1.54	1.44	1.33	1.21
1%	α=.05	5.26	3.80	3.25	2.94	2.75	2.61	2.50	2.42	2.36	2.31	2.23	2.14	2.05	1.95	1.90	1.85	1.79
1%	α=.01	9.51	6.25	5.08	4.47	4.08	3.81	3.62	3.46	3.34	3.24	3.09	2.93	2.77	2.60	2.51	2.41	2.31
	pow .5	5.10	3.18	2.43	2.08	1.81	1.68	1.53	1.47	1.42	1.34	1.25	1.14	1.08	0.96	0.93	0.89	0.85
	pow .8	9.91	6.00	4.56	3.82	3.33	3.02	2.77	2.60	2.47	2.34	2.15	1.96	1.78	1.56	1.46	1.34	1.22
5%	α=.05	8.63	5.30	4.16	3.59	3.25	3.01	2.84	2.71	2.61	2.53	2.41	2.28	2.15	2.02	1.95	1.88	1.81
5%	α=.01	14.43	8.43	6.42	5.41	4.80	4.39	4.09	3.87	3.69	3.55	3.34	3.13	2.91	2.68	2.57	2.45	2.33
	pow .5	8.38	4.58	3.37	2.69	2.35	2.06	1.91	1.74	1.66	1.55	1.42	1.32	1.17	1.03	0.98	0.92	0.87
	pow .8	14.52	7.97	5.79	4.66	4.01	3.54	3.23	2.96	2.79	2.62	2.38	2.16	1.90	1.64	1.52	1.38	1.24
25	nil α=.05	4.23	3.39	2.99	2.76	2.60	2.49	2.40	2.34	2.28	2.24	2.16	2.09	2.01	1.92	1.87	1.82	1.77
	nil α=.01	7.77	5.57	4.68	4.18	3.86	3.63	3.46	3.32	3.22	3.13	2.99	2.85	2.70	2.54	2.45	2.36	2.27
	pow .5	4.08	2.74	2.21	1.87	1.70	1.58	1.45	1.40	1.31	1.29	1.21	1.11	1.01	0.95	0.90	0.84	0.82
	pow .8	8.45	5.41	4.22	3.56	3.15	2.87	2.64	2.49	2.34	2.25	2.08	1.89	1.70	1.52	1.41	1.29	1.18
1%	α=.05	5.27	3.80	3.24	2.93	2.73	2.59	2.49	2.41	2.34	2.29	2.21	2.12	2.03	1.93	1.88	1.83	1.77
1%	α=.01	9.51	6.23	5.05	4.43	4.05	3.78	3.58	3.43	3.31	3.21	3.06	2.90	2.73	2.56	2.47	2.37	2.27
	pow .5	5.12	3.18	2.43	2.07	1.80	1.67	1.52	1.46	1.42	1.33	1.24	1.13	1.03	0.96	0.90	0.87	0.82
	pow .8	9.93	5.99	4.54	3.80	3.31	3.00	2.75	2.58	2.42	2.31	2.13	1.93	1.73	1.53	1.42	1.31	1.18
5%	α=.05	8.74	5.34	4.18	3.60	3.25	3.01	2.84	2.71	2.60	2.52	2.40	2.27	2.14	2.00	1.93	1.86	1.79
5%	α=.01	14.53	8.46	6.42	5.40	4.78	4.37	4.07	3.84	3.67	3.53	3.31	3.10	2.87	2.65	2.53	2.42	2.29
	pow .5	8.49	4.62	3.39	2.70	2.35	2.06	1.91	1.74	1.66	1.54	1.42	1.27	1.17	1.02	0.95	0.90	0.84
	pow .8	14.65	8.02	5.81	4.67	4.00	3.53	3.22	2.95	2.77	2.60	2.36	2.11	1.88	1.62	1.48	1.35	1.20
26	nil α=.05	4.22	3.37	2.98	2.74	2.59	2.47	2.39	2.32	2.26	2.22	2.15	2.07	1.99	1.90	1.85	1.80	1.75
	nil α=.01	7.72	5.53	4.64	4.14	3.82	3.59	3.42	3.29	3.18	3.09	2.96	2.81	2.66	2.50	2.42	2.33	2.23
	pow .5	4.07	2.73	2.20	1.85	1.69	1.52	1.44	1.34	1.30	1.22	1.15	1.10	1.01	0.91	0.86	0.84	0.80
	pow .8	8.42	5.38	4.20	3.53	3.13	2.82	2.62	2.44	2.32	2.20	2.03	1.87	1.68	1.48	1.37	1.27	1.15
1%	α=.05	5.29	3.80	3.23	2.92	2.72	2.58	2.48	2.40	2.33	2.28	2.19	2.11	2.01	1.92	1.86	1.81	1.75
1%	α=.01	9.51	6.21	5.03	4.40	4.01	3.75	3.55	3.39	3.27	3.17	3.02	2.86	2.70	2.52	2.43	2.34	2.24
	pow .5	5.14	3.18	2.42	2.07	1.80	1.66	1.51	1.45	1.35	1.32	1.23	1.12	1.02	0.92	0.90	0.84	0.81
	pow .8	9.95	5.98	4.53	3.78	3.29	2.98	2.73	2.55	2.40	2.29	2.11	1.91	1.71	1.50	1.40	1.28	1.15
5%	α=.05	8.85	5.38	4.20	3.61	3.25	3.01	2.84	2.70	2.60	2.51	2.39	2.26	2.12	1.99	1.92	1.84	1.77
5%	α=.01	14.63	8.48	6.43	5.39	4.77	4.35	4.05	3.82	3.64	3.50	3.29	3.07	2.84	2.62	2.50	2.38	2.26
	pow .5	8.59	4.66	3.41	2.71	2.36	2.06	1.91	1.74	1.66	1.54	1.41	1.26	1.12	1.02	0.95	0.88	0.83
	pow .8	14.78	8.06	5.83	4.67	4.00	3.52	3.21	2.94	2.76	2.58	2.35	2.09	1.84	1.60	1.46	1.32	1.17

Hyp - hypothesis being tested: nil = traditional null; 1% = treatments account for 1% or less of the variance;
5% = treatments account for 5% or less of the variance in outcomes

F for - F values provided for alpha levels of .05 and .01; for traditional null (nil) and minimum-effect (1% and 5%) null hypotheses.
F-equivalent values needed for power of .50 and power of .80 (with α=.05) to reject that hypothesis are also provided

One Stop F Table

	Hyp																		
27	nil α=.05	4.20	3.35	2.96	2.73	2.57	2.46	2.37	2.30	2.25	2.20	2.13	2.05	1.97	1.88	1.84	1.78	1.73
	nil α=.01	7.67	5.49	4.60	4.11	3.78	3.56	3.39	3.26	3.15	3.06	2.93	2.78	2.63	2.47	2.38	2.29	2.20
	pow .5	4.06	2.72	2.19	1.84	1.68	1.51	1.43	1.33	1.29	1.22	1.14	1.09	1.00	0.90	0.86	0.82	0.78
	pow .8	8.40	5.36	4.18	3.51	3.10	2.80	2.60	2.42	2.30	2.18	2.01	1.85	1.66	1.46	1.35	1.24	1.12
1%	α=.05	5.31	3.80	3.22	2.91	2.71	2.57	2.46	2.38	2.32	2.26	2.18	2.09	2.00	1.90	1.85	1.79	1.73
1%	α=.01	9.51	6.19	5.00	4.38	3.99	3.72	3.52	3.37	3.24	3.14	2.99	2.83	2.67	2.49	2.40	2.30	2.20
	pow .5	5.16	3.18	2.42	2.06	1.79	1.65	1.50	1.44	1.34	1.31	1.22	1.11	1.01	0.91	0.86	0.82	0.78
	pow .8	9.98	5.98	4.52	3.77	3.27	2.96	2.71	2.53	2.38	2.27	2.09	1.89	1.69	1.48	1.36	1.25	1.12
5%	α=.05	8.96	5.43	4.22	3.62	3.26	3.01	2.83	2.70	2.59	2.51	2.38	2.25	2.11	1.97	1.90	1.83	1.75
5%	α=.01	14.73	8.51	6.44	5.39	4.76	4.34	4.03	3.80	3.62	3.48	3.26	3.04	2.82	2.59	2.47	2.35	2.22
	pow .5	8.70	4.70	3.43	2.73	2.36	2.06	1.91	1.73	1.65	1.54	1.41	1.26	1.12	0.98	0.91	0.85	0.80
	pow .8	14.91	8.11	5.85	4.68	4.00	3.52	3.20	2.93	2.75	2.57	2.33	2.08	1.82	1.56	1.43	1.29	1.14
28	nil α=.05	4.19	3.34	2.95	2.71	2.56	2.44	2.36	2.29	2.23	2.19	2.12	2.04	1.96	1.87	1.82	1.77	1.71
	nil α=.01	7.63	5.45	4.57	4.07	3.75	3.53	3.36	3.23	3.12	3.03	2.90	2.75	2.60	2.44	2.35	2.26	2.17
	pow .5	4.05	2.71	2.18	1.83	1.67	1.50	1.42	1.32	1.28	1.21	1.13	1.04	0.95	0.90	0.83	0.79	0.77
	pow .8	8.38	5.34	4.15	3.49	3.08	2.78	2.58	2.40	2.28	2.16	1.99	1.81	1.62	1.44	1.32	1.21	1.09
1%	α=.05	5.33	3.80	3.22	2.90	2.70	2.56	2.45	2.37	2.30	2.25	2.17	2.08	1.98	1.89	1.83	1.78	1.72
1%	α=.01	9.52	6.17	4.98	4.35	3.96	3.69	3.49	3.34	3.22	3.12	2.96	2.80	2.64	2.46	2.37	2.27	2.17
	pow .5	5.19	3.19	2.42	2.06	1.78	1.65	1.50	1.43	1.33	1.30	1.17	1.11	1.01	0.91	0.86	0.82	0.77
	pow .8	10.00	5.97	4.50	3.75	3.26	2.94	2.69	2.52	2.36	2.25	2.04	1.87	1.67	1.46	1.34	1.23	1.10
5%	α=.05	9.07	5.47	4.25	3.64	3.26	3.01	2.83	2.70	2.59	2.50	2.37	2.24	2.10	1.96	1.89	1.81	1.73
5%	α=.01	14.83	8.55	6.45	5.39	4.75	4.33	4.02	3.79	3.61	3.46	3.24	3.02	2.79	2.56	2.44	2.32	2.19
	pow .5	8.80	4.74	3.45	2.74	2.37	2.07	1.91	1.74	1.59	1.54	1.41	1.25	1.11	0.98	0.91	0.85	0.78
	pow .8	15.04	8.16	5.87	4.69	4.00	3.52	3.19	2.92	2.71	2.56	2.32	2.06	1.81	1.54	1.41	1.27	1.12
29	nil α=.05	4.18	3.33	2.93	2.70	2.54	2.43	2.35	2.28	2.22	2.18	2.10	2.03	1.94	1.85	1.80	1.75	1.70
	nil α=.01	7.60	5.42	4.54	4.04	3.73	3.50	3.33	3.20	3.09	3.00	2.87	2.73	2.57	2.41	2.32	2.23	2.14
	pow .5	4.04	2.70	2.17	1.83	1.66	1.49	1.42	1.31	1.28	1.20	1.13	1.03	0.95	0.86	0.82	0.79	0.74
	pow .8	8.35	5.32	4.14	3.47	3.06	2.76	2.56	2.38	2.26	2.14	1.97	1.79	1.60	1.40	1.30	1.19	1.07
1%	α=.05	5.35	3.80	3.21	2.89	2.69	2.55	2.44	2.36	2.29	2.24	2.15	2.07	1.97	1.87	1.82	1.76	1.70
1%	α=.01	9.53	6.16	4.96	4.33	3.94	3.67	3.47	3.31	3.19	3.09	2.94	2.78	2.61	2.44	2.34	2.25	2.14
	pow .5	5.21	3.19	2.41	2.05	1.78	1.64	1.49	1.43	1.33	1.24	1.16	1.10	1.00	0.90	0.83	0.79	0.75
	pow .8	10.03	5.97	4.49	3.74	3.24	2.93	2.67	2.50	2.34	2.21	2.03	1.85	1.65	1.44	1.31	1.20	1.07
5%	α=.05	9.18	5.52	4.27	3.65	3.27	3.02	2.83	2.69	2.59	2.50	2.36	2.23	2.09	1.95	1.87	1.80	1.72
5%	α=.01	14.93	8.58	6.46	5.39	4.75	4.32	4.01	3.77	3.59	3.44	3.22	3.00	2.77	2.53	2.41	2.29	2.16
	pow .5	8.91	4.78	3.47	2.75	2.38	2.07	1.91	1.74	1.59	1.54	1.40	1.25	1.11	0.97	0.91	0.82	0.77
	pow .8	15.17	8.21	5.89	4.70	4.01	3.51	3.19	2.91	2.70	2.55	2.31	2.05	1.79	1.53	1.39	1.24	1.09

Hyp - hypothesis being tested: nil = traditional null; 1% = treatments account for 1% or less of the variance;
5% = treatments account for 5% or less of the variance in outcomes

F for - F values provided for alpha levels of .05 and .01; for traditional null (nil) and minimum-effect (1% and 5%) null hypotheses.
F-equivalent values needed for power of .50 and power of .80 (with α=.05) to reject that hypothesis are also provided

One Stop F Table

df	Hyp	stat																	
30	nil	α=.05	4.16	3.32	2.92	2.69	2.53	2.42	2.33	2.27	2.21	2.16	2.09	2.01	1.93	1.84	1.79	1.74	1.68
	nil	α=.01	7.56	5.39	4.51	4.02	3.70	3.47	3.30	3.17	3.07	2.98	2.84	2.70	2.55	2.39	2.30	2.21	2.11
		pow .5	4.03	2.69	2.16	1.82	1.65	1.48	1.41	1.30	1.27	1.19	1.12	1.02	0.94	0.86	0.82	0.76	0.73
		pow .8	8.33	5.30	4.12	3.45	3.05	2.74	2.54	2.36	2.24	2.12	1.95	1.77	1.58	1.39	1.28	1.17	1.04
	1%	α=.05	5.38	3.80	3.21	2.89	2.68	2.54	2.43	2.35	2.28	2.23	2.14	2.05	1.96	1.86	1.80	1.75	1.69
	1%	α=.01	9.54	6.15	4.94	4.31	3.92	3.64	3.44	3.29	3.17	3.07	2.91	2.75	2.59	2.41	2.32	2.22	2.12
		pow .5	5.23	3.19	2.41	2.05	1.77	1.64	1.49	1.42	1.32	1.24	1.15	1.05	0.96	0.87	0.82	0.77	0.73
		pow .8	10.06	5.97	4.49	3.73	3.23	2.91	2.66	2.49	2.32	2.19	2.01	1.81	1.61	1.41	1.30	1.17	1.05
	5%	α=.05	9.29	5.57	4.29	3.66	3.28	3.02	2.83	2.69	2.58	2.49	2.36	2.22	2.08	1.94	1.86	1.78	1.70
	5%	α=.01	15.04	8.62	6.47	5.40	4.75	4.31	4.00	3.76	3.58	3.43	3.20	2.98	2.75	2.51	2.39	2.27	2.14
		pow .5	9.01	4.82	3.50	2.76	2.39	2.08	1.92	1.74	1.59	1.54	1.40	1.25	1.11	0.94	0.88	0.82	0.76
		pow .8	15.31	8.26	5.91	4.71	4.01	3.51	3.19	2.91	2.69	2.54	2.30	2.04	1.78	1.50	1.36	1.23	1.07
40	nil	α=.05	4.08	3.23	2.84	2.61	2.45	2.34	2.25	2.18	2.12	2.08	2.00	1.92	1.84	1.74	1.69	1.64	1.58
	nil	α=.01	7.31	5.18	4.31	3.83	3.51	3.29	3.12	2.99	2.89	2.80	2.66	2.52	2.37	2.20	2.11	2.02	1.92
		pow .5	3.97	2.63	2.02	1.76	1.52	1.42	1.29	1.25	1.16	1.08	1.02	0.93	0.86	0.76	0.70	0.65	0.61
		pow .8	8.20	5.16	3.96	3.32	2.89	2.61	2.39	2.23	2.09	1.97	1.80	1.62	1.44	1.25	1.12	1.00	0.88
	1%	α=.05	5.64	3.85	3.21	2.86	2.64	2.49	2.38	2.29	2.22	2.16	2.07	1.97	1.87	1.77	1.71	1.65	1.58
	1%	α=.01	9.75	6.12	4.86	4.20	3.79	3.51	3.30	3.14	3.01	2.91	2.75	2.59	2.42	2.23	2.14	2.03	1.92
		pow .5	5.49	3.26	2.42	2.04	1.75	1.54	1.45	1.33	1.22	1.20	1.12	1.01	0.88	0.77	0.71	0.66	0.61
		pow .8	10.38	6.01	4.46	3.67	3.15	2.80	2.56	2.36	2.19	2.08	1.90	1.70	1.48	1.25	1.14	1.01	0.88
	5%	α=.05	10.44	6.01	4.56	3.83	3.39	3.09	2.88	2.72	2.59	2.49	2.34	2.19	2.03	1.86	1.78	1.69	1.60
	5%	α=.01	16.14	9.06	6.70	5.51	4.80	4.32	3.98	3.72	3.52	3.35	3.11	2.86	2.61	2.36	2.22	2.09	1.95
		pow .5	10.00	5.35	3.73	3.00	2.49	2.15	1.97	1.77	1.61	1.55	1.35	1.19	1.05	0.88	0.80	0.72	0.63
		pow .8	16.64	8.82	6.19	4.91	4.10	3.56	3.20	2.90	2.67	2.51	2.22	1.94	1.67	1.38	1.23	1.07	0.91
50	nil	α=.05	4.03	3.18	2.79	2.56	2.40	2.29	2.20	2.13	2.07	2.02	1.95	1.87	1.78	1.68	1.63	1.57	1.51
	nil	α=.01	7.17	5.06	4.20	3.72	3.41	3.19	3.02	2.89	2.78	2.70	2.56	2.42	2.26	2.10	2.01	1.91	1.80
		pow .5	3.93	2.59	1.99	1.72	1.49	1.39	1.26	1.15	1.13	1.06	0.99	0.91	0.79	0.70	0.63	0.60	0.54
		pow .8	8.11	5.09	3.88	3.25	2.82	2.54	2.31	2.13	2.01	1.89	1.73	1.55	1.35	1.14	1.02	0.91	0.78
	1%	α=.05	5.93	3.94	3.24	2.87	2.63	2.47	2.35	2.26	2.19	2.12	2.03	1.93	1.83	1.71	1.65	1.59	1.52
	1%	α=.01	10.04	6.18	4.85	4.16	3.74	3.44	3.23	3.07	2.94	2.83	2.67	2.50	2.32	2.13	2.03	1.92	1.81
		pow .5	5.76	3.35	2.46	1.97	1.75	1.54	1.44	1.32	1.21	1.18	1.04	0.94	0.81	0.71	0.67	0.60	0.54
		pow .8	10.74	6.11	4.48	3.63	3.13	2.76	2.52	2.31	2.14	2.03	1.82	1.61	1.39	1.17	1.05	0.92	0.78
	5%	α=.05	11.39	6.50	4.84	4.02	3.53	3.20	2.96	2.78	2.64	2.53	2.36	2.19	2.01	1.83	1.74	1.64	1.54
	5%	α=.01	17.26	9.56	6.98	5.69	4.92	4.40	4.03	3.75	3.53	3.35	3.09	2.82	2.55	2.28	2.14	1.99	1.84
		pow .5	11.09	5.76	4.08	3.16	2.61	2.23	2.03	1.82	1.65	1.58	1.37	1.20	1.00	0.84	0.76	0.66	0.57
		pow .8	17.86	9.36	6.55	5.11	4.24	3.66	3.27	2.95	2.70	2.53	2.22	1.92	1.61	1.31	1.16	0.99	0.81

Hyp - hypothesis being tested: nil = traditional null; 1% = treatments account for 1% or less of the variance; 5% = reatments account for 5% or less of the variance in outcomes

F for - F values provided for alpha levels of .05 and .01; for traditional null (nil) and minimum-effect (1% and 5%) null hypotheses. F-equivalent values needed for power of .50 and power of .80 (with α=.05) to reject that hypothesis are also provided

One Stop F Table

	Hyp																	
60	nil α=.05	3.99	3.15	2.76	2.53	2.37	2.25	2.17	2.10	2.04	1.99	1.92	1.83	1.75	1.65	1.59	1.53	1.47
	nil α=.01	7.07	4.98	4.13	3.65	3.34	3.12	2.95	2.82	2.72	2.63	2.50	2.35	2.20	2.03	1.94	1.84	1.73
	pow .5	3.90	2.57	1.97	1.70	1.47	1.30	1.24	1.13	1.04	0.91	0.84	0.78	0.65	0.58	0.54	0.48	
	pow .8	8.06	5.04	3.83	3.20	2.77	2.46	2.26	2.08	1.94	1.85	1.66	1.48	1.30	1.08	0.96	0.84	0.70
	1% α=.05	6.24	4.04	3.29	2.90	2.64	2.47	2.35	2.25	2.17	2.11	2.01	1.91	1.80	1.68	1.62	1.55	1.47
	1% α=.01	10.35	6.28	4.88	4.16	3.72	3.42	3.20	3.03	2.90	2.79	2.62	2.45	2.26	2.07	1.96	1.85	1.73
	pow .5	6.04	3.44	2.50	1.99	1.76	1.54	1.37	1.31	1.20	1.11	1.03	0.93	0.80	0.70	0.63	0.55	0.50
	pow .8	11.13	6.22	4.53	3.65	3.13	2.75	2.47	2.29	2.11	1.97	1.78	1.58	1.35	1.13	0.99	0.86	0.72
	5% α=.05	12.49	6.94	5.14	4.23	3.68	3.31	3.05	2.86	2.70	2.58	2.39	2.20	2.01	1.82	1.72	1.61	1.50
	5% α=.01	18.38	10.06	7.29	5.90	5.07	4.51	4.11	3.81	3.58	3.39	3.11	2.82	2.53	2.24	2.09	1.93	1.77
	pow .5	11.97	6.30	4.33	3.33	2.82	2.41	2.11	1.88	1.77	1.62	1.39	1.21	1.01	0.84	0.72	0.61	0.53
	pow .8	19.10	9.93	6.86	5.33	4.44	3.81	3.36	3.02	2.78	2.57	2.24	1.93	1.60	1.29	1.11	0.93	0.75
70	nil α=.05	3.97	3.13	2.74	2.50	2.35	2.23	2.14	2.07	2.01	1.97	1.89	1.81	1.72	1.62	1.56	1.50	1.43
	nil α=.01	7.01	4.92	4.07	3.60	3.29	3.07	2.91	2.78	2.67	2.58	2.45	2.30	2.15	1.98	1.89	1.78	1.67
	pow .5	3.88	2.55	1.95	1.68	1.46	1.28	1.23	1.12	1.03	1.02	0.90	0.82	0.72	0.60	0.58	0.51	0.45
	pow .8	8.02	5.00	3.80	3.16	2.73	2.43	2.23	2.05	1.91	1.81	1.62	1.44	1.24	1.03	0.92	0.80	0.66
	1% α=.05	6.57	4.14	3.35	2.92	2.66	2.48	2.35	2.25	2.17	2.10	2.00	1.89	1.78	1.66	1.59	1.52	1.44
	1% α=.01	10.67	6.39	4.93	4.18	3.73	3.41	3.19	3.01	2.87	2.76	2.59	2.41	2.23	2.03	1.92	1.80	1.68
	pow .5	6.32	3.54	2.55	2.11	1.78	1.55	1.37	1.32	1.20	1.11	1.03	0.93	0.80	0.66	0.59	0.52	0.45
	pow .8	11.55	6.35	4.59	3.71	3.14	2.75	2.47	2.28	2.10	1.96	1.76	1.55	1.32	1.08	0.95	0.81	0.66
	5% α=.05	13.34	7.42	5.45	4.43	3.84	3.44	3.16	2.94	2.77	2.64	2.44	2.23	2.03	1.81	1.71	1.59	1.48
	5% α=.01	19.46	10.58	7.61	6.13	5.23	4.64	4.21	3.89	3.64	3.44	3.14	2.84	2.53	2.22	2.06	1.89	1.72
	pow .5	13.03	6.69	4.56	3.60	2.94	2.50	2.18	2.02	1.82	1.66	1.49	1.23	1.02	0.80	0.72	0.61	0.50
	pow .8	20.22	10.46	7.20	5.59	4.60	3.93	3.45	3.13	2.84	2.62	2.30	1.94	1.60	1.26	1.09	0.90	0.71
80	nil α=.05	3.95	3.11	2.72	2.49	2.33	2.21	2.12	2.05	2.00	1.95	1.87	1.79	1.70	1.60	1.54	1.48	1.41
	nil α=.01	6.96	4.88	4.04	3.56	3.26	3.04	2.87	2.74	2.64	2.55	2.41	2.27	2.11	1.94	1.85	1.75	1.63
	pow .5	3.87	2.54	1.94	1.67	1.44	1.27	1.21	1.11	1.02	0.94	0.89	0.82	0.71	0.60	0.54	0.48	0.42
	pow .8	7.99	4.97	3.77	3.14	2.71	2.40	2.20	2.02	1.88	1.76	1.60	1.42	1.22	1.00	0.88	0.76	0.62
	1% α=.05	6.83	4.26	3.41	2.96	2.69	2.50	2.36	2.26	2.17	2.10	2.00	1.89	1.77	1.64	1.57	1.50	1.42
	1% α=.01	10.98	6.51	4.99	4.22	3.74	3.42	3.19	3.01	2.86	2.75	2.57	2.39	2.20	1.99	1.89	1.77	1.64
	pow .5	6.73	3.64	2.60	2.14	1.80	1.56	1.38	1.32	1.21	1.11	1.03	0.87	0.79	0.65	0.58	0.52	0.44
	pow .8	11.95	6.48	4.66	3.75	3.16	2.76	2.47	2.28	2.10	1.95	1.75	1.52	1.31	1.06	0.93	0.79	0.63
	5% α=.05	14.39	7.84	5.71	4.65	4.01	3.58	3.26	3.03	2.85	2.71	2.49	2.27	2.04	1.82	1.70	1.58	1.46
	5% α=.01	20.52	11.08	7.93	6.35	5.41	4.77	4.32	3.98	3.72	3.50	3.18	2.86	2.54	2.21	2.04	1.87	1.69
	pow .5	13.83	7.22	4.92	3.76	3.06	2.59	2.34	2.08	1.87	1.70	1.52	1.25	1.03	0.80	0.69	0.58	0.47
	pow .8	21.36	11.02	7.55	5.81	4.76	4.06	3.59	3.21	2.91	2.67	2.34	1.97	1.61	1.25	1.06	0.88	0.67

Hyp - hypothesis being tested: nil = traditional null; 1% = treatments account for 1% or less of the variance;
5% = treatments account for 5% or less of the variance in outcomes

F for - F values provided for alpha levels of .05 and .01; for traditional null (nil) and minimum-effect (1% and 5%) null hypotheses.
F-equivalent values needed for power of .50 and power of .80 (with α=.05) to reject that hypothesis are also provided

108

One Stop F Table

Hyp																		
90																		
nil α=.05	3.94	3.10	2.71	2.47	2.32	2.20	2.11	2.04	1.98	1.94	1.86	1.78	1.69	1.58	1.53	1.46	1.39
nil α=.01	6.92	4.85	4.01	3.53	3.23	3.01	2.84	2.72	2.61	2.52	2.39	2.24	2.09	1.91	1.82	1.72	1.60
pow .5	3.86	2.53	1.93	1.66	1.43	1.26	1.21	1.10	1.01	0.94	0.89	0.81	0.70	0.59	0.54	0.46	0.40
pow .8	7.97	4.95	3.75	3.12	2.69	2.38	2.18	2.00	1.86	1.74	1.58	1.40	1.20	0.98	0.86	0.73	0.59
1% α=.05	6.97	4.37	3.48	3.00	2.71	2.52	2.38	2.26	2.18	2.11	2.00	1.88	1.76	1.63	1.56	1.48	1.40
1% α=.01	11.29	6.64	5.06	4.26	3.77	3.43	3.19	3.01	2.86	2.74	2.56	2.38	2.18	1.97	1.86	1.74	1.61
pow .5	6.86	3.74	2.66	2.18	1.83	1.58	1.47	1.33	1.21	1.12	1.03	0.87	0.79	0.65	0.55	0.49	0.40
pow .8	12.12	6.62	4.74	3.79	3.19	2.78	2.52	2.28	2.10	1.95	1.75	1.51	1.29	1.04	0.89	0.76	0.60
5% α=.05	15.17	8.31	6.02	4.88	4.15	3.70	3.37	3.12	2.93	2.77	2.54	2.30	2.07	1.83	1.70	1.58	1.44
5% α=.01	21.57	11.59	8.25	6.59	5.58	4.92	4.44	4.08	3.80	3.57	3.24	2.90	2.55	2.21	2.03	1.85	1.66
pow .5	14.87	7.58	5.14	3.92	3.29	2.78	2.41	2.14	1.92	1.82	1.55	1.34	1.09	0.85	0.69	0.58	0.45
pow .8	22.43	11.51	7.87	6.04	4.97	4.23	3.70	3.30	2.99	2.77	2.39	2.03	1.65	1.27	1.06	0.87	0.65
100																		
nil α=.05	3.93	3.09	2.70	2.46	2.30	2.19	2.10	2.03	1.97	1.92	1.85	1.77	1.67	1.57	1.51	1.45	1.37
nil α=.01	6.89	4.82	3.98	3.51	3.21	2.99	2.82	2.69	2.59	2.50	2.37	2.22	2.07	1.89	1.80	1.69	1.57
pow .5	3.85	2.52	1.92	1.66	1.43	1.26	1.20	1.10	1.01	0.93	0.88	0.80	0.70	0.59	0.50	0.46	0.39
pow .8	7.95	4.94	3.73	3.10	2.67	2.37	2.17	1.99	1.84	1.72	1.56	1.38	1.18	0.97	0.83	0.71	0.57
1% α=.05	7.24	4.49	3.55	3.04	2.74	2.54	2.39	2.28	2.19	2.11	2.00	1.88	1.76	1.62	1.55	1.47	1.38
1% α=.01	11.60	6.76	5.13	4.30	3.80	3.45	3.21	3.02	2.87	2.75	2.56	2.37	2.17	1.96	1.84	1.72	1.58
pow .5	7.11	3.84	2.71	2.22	1.85	1.59	1.49	1.34	1.22	1.12	1.04	0.87	0.74	0.61	0.55	0.49	0.39
pow .8	12.45	6.76	4.82	3.83	3.22	2.80	2.53	2.29	2.11	1.95	1.75	1.50	1.26	1.01	0.88	0.74	0.58
5% α=.05	16.18	8.81	6.27	5.05	4.32	3.83	3.49	3.21	3.00	2.84	2.60	2.34	2.09	1.84	1.71	1.57	1.43
5% α=.01	22.59	12.08	8.57	6.82	5.76	5.06	4.56	4.18	3.88	3.65	3.29	2.94	2.58	2.21	2.03	1.84	1.64
pow .5	15.62	7.93	5.51	4.19	3.40	2.87	2.49	2.29	2.06	1.87	1.58	1.36	1.11	0.86	0.70	0.59	0.44
pow .8	23.49	12.03	8.22	6.30	5.14	4.36	3.81	3.43	3.10	2.83	2.43	2.06	1.67	1.28	1.06	0.86	0.63
120																		
nil α=.05	3.91	3.07	2.68	2.45	2.29	2.17	2.09	2.01	1.96	1.91	1.83	1.75	1.66	1.55	1.49	1.43	1.35
nil α=.01	6.85	4.79	3.95	3.48	3.17	2.96	2.79	2.66	2.56	2.47	2.34	2.19	2.03	1.86	1.76	1.65	1.53
pow .5	3.84	2.51	1.91	1.56	1.42	1.25	1.11	1.09	1.00	0.92	0.87	0.74	0.64	0.54	0.50	0.43	0.36
pow .8	7.93	4.91	3.71	3.05	2.65	2.34	2.12	1.97	1.82	1.70	1.54	1.34	1.14	0.92	0.81	0.68	0.53
1% α=.05	7.76	4.74	3.66	3.13	2.81	2.59	2.43	2.31	2.21	2.13	2.01	1.89	1.75	1.61	1.54	1.45	1.36
1% α=.01	12.20	7.02	5.28	4.40	3.86	3.50	3.24	3.04	2.88	2.76	2.56	2.36	2.15	1.93	1.81	1.69	1.55
pow .5	7.58	4.04	2.92	2.29	1.90	1.63	1.52	1.36	1.24	1.13	1.05	0.87	0.74	0.61	0.54	0.46	0.37
pow .8	13.10	7.05	4.98	3.93	3.29	2.85	2.56	2.32	2.12	1.97	1.75	1.50	1.25	1.00	0.86	0.71	0.55
5% α=.05	17.88	9.64	6.89	5.45	4.64	4.09	3.70	3.41	3.17	2.98	2.71	2.43	2.15	1.87	1.72	1.57	1.42
5% α=.01	24.59	13.05	9.20	7.28	6.12	5.35	4.80	4.38	4.06	3.80	3.41	3.02	2.63	2.23	2.03	1.83	1.61
pow .5	17.37	8.79	5.92	4.63	3.74	3.15	2.73	2.41	2.25	2.04	1.72	1.47	1.13	0.87	0.74	0.59	0.42
pow .8	25.54	13.02	8.83	6.78	5.51	4.67	4.06	3.61	3.30	3.00	2.57	2.16	1.71	1.29	1.08	0.85	0.61

Hyp - hypothesis being tested: nil = traditional null; 1% = treatments account for 1% or less of the variance; 5% = reatments account for 5% or less of the variance in outcomes

F for - F values provided for alpha levels of .05 and .01; for traditional null (nil) and minimum-effect (1% and 5%) null hypotheses. F-equivalent values needed for power of .50 and power of .80 (with α=.05) to reject that hypothesis are also provided

One Stop F Table

n	Hyp																			
150	nil	α=.05	3.89	3.06	2.67	2.43	2.27	2.16	2.07	2.00	1.94	1.89	1.81	1.73	1.64	1.53	1.47	1.40	1.32
	nil	α=.01	6.80	4.75	3.92	3.45	3.14	2.92	2.76	2.63	2.53	2.44	2.30	2.16	2.00	1.83	1.73	1.62	1.49
		pow.5	3.83	2.50	1.90	1.55	1.41	1.24	1.10	1.08	0.99	0.92	0.86	0.73	0.63	0.54	0.45	0.40	0.33
		pow.8	7.90	4.89	3.69	3.02	2.63	2.32	2.09	1.94	1.80	1.68	1.52	1.31	1.11	0.90	0.77	0.64	0.49
	1%	α=.05	8.61	5.01	3.86	3.28	2.92	2.66	2.49	2.36	2.25	2.17	2.03	1.90	1.76	1.61	1.53	1.44	1.34
	1%	α=.01	13.04	7.40	5.51	4.56	3.98	3.59	3.31	3.09	2.93	2.79	2.58	2.37	2.15	1.92	1.79	1.66	1.51
		pow.5	8.26	4.42	3.09	2.40	1.98	1.78	1.56	1.40	1.27	1.15	1.06	0.88	0.74	0.61	0.51	0.43	0.34
		pow.8	14.11	7.43	5.21	4.09	3.40	2.96	2.62	2.37	2.16	2.00	1.77	1.51	1.25	0.98	0.83	0.68	0.51
	5%	α=.05	20.52	10.86	7.64	6.06	5.11	4.48	4.03	3.69	3.41	3.20	2.88	2.57	2.24	1.92	1.75	1.59	1.41
	5%	α=.01	27.47	14.46	10.12	7.95	6.65	5.78	5.16	4.69	4.33	4.04	3.60	3.17	2.73	2.28	2.06	1.83	1.59
		pow.5	19.73	10.24	6.86	5.19	4.19	3.52	3.04	2.67	2.48	2.25	1.90	1.61	1.23	0.93	0.75	0.59	0.41
		pow.8	28.49	14.57	9.81	7.46	6.05	5.10	4.43	3.92	3.56	3.24	2.76	2.31	1.81	1.35	1.09	0.85	0.58
200	nil	α=.05	3.88	3.04	2.65	2.42	2.26	2.14	2.05	1.98	1.93	1.88	1.80	1.71	1.62	1.51	1.45	1.38	1.30
	nil	α=.01	6.76	4.71	3.88	3.41	3.11	2.89	2.73	2.60	2.50	2.41	2.27	2.13	1.97	1.79	1.69	1.58	1.45
		pow.5	3.82	2.48	1.89	1.54	1.40	1.23	1.09	1.07	0.98	0.91	0.79	0.72	0.63	0.49	0.45	0.37	0.30
		pow.8	7.88	4.86	3.66	3.00	2.60	2.30	2.07	1.92	1.78	1.65	1.47	1.29	1.09	0.86	0.75	0.60	0.45
	1%	α=.05	9.58	5.57	4.22	3.49	3.08	2.81	2.61	2.46	2.33	2.23	2.09	1.93	1.78	1.61	1.52	1.43	1.32
	1%	α=.01	14.39	8.02	5.90	4.83	4.18	3.75	3.43	3.20	3.01	2.86	2.63	2.40	2.16	1.91	1.78	1.64	1.48
		pow.5	9.37	4.88	3.36	2.68	2.20	1.88	1.64	1.46	1.40	1.28	1.09	0.96	0.75	0.61	0.51	0.43	0.33
		pow.8	15.40	8.08	5.62	4.38	3.62	3.11	2.74	2.46	2.27	2.09	1.81	1.56	1.26	0.98	0.82	0.66	0.48
	5%	α=.05	24.55	12.87	8.94	7.02	5.88	5.11	4.56	4.15	3.84	3.56	3.18	2.79	2.40	2.01	1.82	1.62	1.41
	5%	α=.01	32.04	16.72	11.60	8.94	7.51	6.49	5.76	5.21	4.78	4.44	3.93	3.42	2.90	2.38	2.12	1.85	1.58
		pow.5	23.65	11.85	9.04	6.17	4.96	4.16	3.58	3.15	2.81	2.53	2.21	1.79	1.42	1.01	0.81	0.63	0.41
		pow.8	33.10	16.67	11.31	8.57	6.92	5.82	5.04	4.45	3.99	3.61	3.10	2.54	2.00	1.44	1.15	0.88	0.58
300	nil	α=.05	3.86	3.03	2.63	2.40	2.24	2.13	2.04	1.97	1.91	1.86	1.78	1.70	1.60	1.49	1.43	1.36	1.27
	nil	α=.01	6.72	4.68	3.85	3.38	3.08	2.86	2.70	2.57	2.47	2.38	2.24	2.10	1.94	1.76	1.66	1.55	1.41
		pow.5	3.80	2.47	1.88	1.53	1.39	1.22	1.09	0.98	0.97	0.90	0.78	0.72	0.62	0.48	0.41	0.37	0.26
		pow.8	7.85	4.84	3.64	2.98	2.58	2.28	2.05	1.87	1.75	1.63	1.44	1.27	1.07	0.83	0.71	0.58	0.41
	1%	α=.05	11.62	6.54	4.85	3.97	3.43	3.08	2.84	2.65	2.51	2.38	2.20	2.02	1.83	1.64	1.54	1.43	1.31
	1%	α=.01	16.85	9.18	6.63	5.36	4.59	4.07	3.70	3.42	3.20	3.03	2.76	2.49	2.22	1.93	1.78	1.62	1.45
		pow.5	11.36	5.83	3.97	3.17	2.56	2.17	1.89	1.67	1.50	1.45	1.23	1.01	0.84	0.62	0.51	0.43	0.30
		pow.8	17.91	9.26	6.37	4.96	4.04	3.44	3.02	2.69	2.44	2.27	1.95	1.63	1.33	1.00	0.82	0.66	0.45
	5%	α=.05	32.04	16.65	11.52	8.94	7.35	6.32	5.59	5.05	4.62	4.28	3.77	3.25	2.74	2.22	1.97	1.70	1.44
	5%	α=.01	40.62	20.94	14.40	11.13	9.16	7.86	6.92	6.21	5.67	5.23	4.58	3.92	3.26	2.60	2.27	1.94	1.59
		pow.5	31.22	15.66	10.47	7.87	6.49	5.42	4.66	4.09	3.64	3.29	2.75	2.29	1.73	1.22	0.96	0.70	0.43
		pow.8	41.71	20.99	14.09	10.62	8.63	7.22	6.23	5.48	4.90	4.43	3.73	3.07	2.35	1.66	1.31	0.96	0.59

Hyp - hypothesis being tested: nil = traditional null; 1% = treatments account for 1% or less of the variance;
  5% = reatments account for 5% or less of the variance in outcomes

F for - F values provided for alpha levels of .05 and .01; for traditional null (nil) and minimum-effect (1% and 5%) null hypotheses.
  F-equivalent values needed for power of .50 and power of .80 (with α=.05) to reject that hypothesis are also provided

One Stop F Table

	Hyp																		
400	nil α=.05	3.85	3.02	2.63	2.39	2.24	2.12	2.03	1.96	1.90	1.85	1.77	1.69	1.59	1.48	1.42	1.35	1.26
	nil α=.01	6.70	4.66	3.83	3.37	3.06	2.85	2.68	2.56	2.45	2.36	2.23	2.08	1.92	1.74	1.64	1.53	1.39
	pow .5	3.80	2.47	1.88	1.52	1.38	1.21	1.08	0.97	0.97	0.90	0.78	0.71	0.62	0.48	0.41	0.34	0.25
	pow .8	7.84	4.83	3.63	2.96	2.57	2.26	2.04	1.86	1.74	1.62	1.43	1.25	1.06	0.82	0.69	0.55	0.39
	1% α=.05	13.49	7.44	5.43	4.42	3.78	3.35	3.07	2.85	2.68	2.54	2.32	2.11	1.90	1.68	1.56	1.44	1.30
	1% α=.01	19.02	10.26	7.33	5.87	4.98	4.39	3.97	3.65	3.40	3.20	2.90	2.60	2.29	1.97	1.80	1.63	1.44
	pow .5	13.21	6.73	4.56	3.47	2.79	2.46	2.14	1.89	1.70	1.54	1.38	1.12	0.92	0.68	0.56	0.43	0.30
	pow .8	20.18	10.35	7.07	5.42	4.40	3.77	3.29	2.93	2.65	2.42	2.10	1.75	1.41	1.04	0.86	0.66	0.44
	5% α=.05	39.07	20.15	13.84	10.68	8.79	7.53	6.62	5.95	5.42	4.98	4.33	3.71	3.08	2.44	2.12	1.80	1.48
	5% α=.01	48.68	24.94	17.05	13.11	10.74	9.16	8.04	7.19	6.53	6.00	5.21	4.42	3.63	2.84	2.44	2.04	1.63
	pow .5	38.66	19.38	12.95	9.73	7.80	6.51	5.59	4.90	4.36	4.04	3.37	2.71	2.04	1.42	1.11	0.80	0.48
	pow .8	49.91	25.07	16.78	12.64	10.16	8.50	7.32	6.43	5.73	5.24	4.39	3.55	2.71	1.88	1.47	1.06	0.63
500	nil α=.05	3.85	3.01	2.62	2.39	2.23	2.12	2.03	1.95	1.90	1.85	1.77	1.68	1.59	1.48	1.41	1.34	1.25
	nil α=.01	6.68	4.65	3.82	3.36	3.05	2.84	2.67	2.55	2.44	2.36	2.22	2.07	1.91	1.73	1.63	1.52	1.38
	pow .5	3.79	2.46	1.87	1.52	1.38	1.21	1.08	0.97	0.97	0.89	0.77	0.71	0.56	0.48	0.41	0.34	0.25
	pow .8	7.83	4.82	3.62	2.96	2.56	2.26	2.03	1.85	1.73	1.61	1.42	1.25	1.03	0.82	0.69	0.55	0.38
	1% α=.05	15.23	8.29	5.98	4.82	4.13	3.65	3.29	3.04	2.84	2.69	2.45	2.21	1.97	1.72	1.59	1.45	1.30
	1% α=.01	21.10	11.28	8.00	6.36	5.37	4.70	4.23	3.88	3.60	3.38	3.04	2.71	2.36	2.01	1.83	1.64	1.43
	pow .5	14.99	7.61	5.14	3.90	3.15	2.64	2.38	2.10	1.89	1.71	1.44	1.24	0.95	0.69	0.56	0.44	0.30
	pow .8	22.31	11.39	7.74	5.91	4.81	4.06	3.57	3.16	2.85	2.60	2.22	1.86	1.46	1.07	0.87	0.67	0.44
	5% α=.05	46.31	23.76	16.24	12.45	10.16	8.63	7.57	6.77	6.15	5.65	4.91	4.16	3.40	2.66	2.28	1.90	1.52
	5% α=.01	56.40	28.82	19.60	15.02	12.26	10.43	9.11	8.13	7.36	6.75	5.83	4.91	3.99	3.07	2.61	2.14	1.67
	pow .5	45.18	22.62	15.10	11.32	9.05	7.54	6.65	5.82	5.18	4.67	3.90	3.13	2.42	1.62	1.26	0.90	0.52
	pow .8	57.52	28.85	19.30	14.50	11.61	9.68	8.44	7.40	6.60	5.96	4.99	4.03	3.09	2.11	1.64	1.17	0.67
600	nil α=.05	3.85	3.01	2.62	2.39	2.23	2.11	2.02	1.95	1.89	1.84	1.77	1.68	1.58	1.47	1.41	1.34	1.25
	nil α=.01	6.67	4.64	3.81	3.35	3.05	2.83	2.67	2.54	2.44	2.35	2.21	2.07	1.91	1.73	1.63	1.51	1.37
	pow .5	3.79	2.46	1.87	1.52	1.38	1.21	1.08	0.97	0.96	0.89	0.77	0.71	0.56	0.48	0.41	0.34	0.25
	pow .8	7.82	4.82	3.62	2.95	2.56	2.25	2.02	1.85	1.73	1.61	1.42	1.24	1.02	0.81	0.68	0.54	0.38
	1% α=.05	16.94	9.11	6.51	5.21	4.43	3.91	3.54	3.24	3.01	2.84	2.57	2.31	2.03	1.76	1.62	1.47	1.31
	1% α=.01	23.08	12.25	8.64	6.83	5.74	5.01	4.49	4.10	3.80	3.55	3.18	2.81	2.44	2.06	1.86	1.66	1.44
	pow .5	16.14	8.46	5.71	4.32	3.49	2.93	2.52	2.32	2.07	1.88	1.59	1.28	1.04	0.75	0.61	0.47	0.30
	pow .8	24.06	12.38	8.38	6.38	5.18	4.38	3.80	3.41	3.05	2.78	2.37	1.95	1.55	1.13	0.91	0.69	0.44
	5% α=.05	52.82	26.98	18.38	14.08	11.50	9.78	8.55	7.63	6.91	6.34	5.48	4.59	3.73	2.86	2.44	2.00	1.56
	5% α=.01	63.87	32.55	22.11	16.89	13.75	11.65	10.16	9.05	8.18	7.48	6.44	5.39	4.35	3.30	2.78	2.25	1.72
	pow .5	52.51	26.28	17.54	13.17	10.55	8.80	7.55	6.61	5.88	5.30	4.42	3.63	2.73	1.88	1.41	1.00	0.57
	pow .8	65.29	32.72	21.87	16.44	13.19	11.02	9.47	8.30	7.40	6.67	5.59	4.54	3.44	2.37	1.80	1.27	0.72

Hyp - hypothesis being tested: nil = traditional null; 1% = treatments account for 1% or less of the variance; 5% = reatments account for 5% or less of the variance in outcomes

F for - F values provided for alpha levels of .05 and .01; for traditional null (nil) and minimum-effect (1% and 5%) null hypotheses. F-equivalent values needed for power of .50 and power of .80 (with α=.05) to reject that hypothesis are also provided

One Stop F Table

		1	2	3	4	5	6	7	8	9	10	11	12	13	14	15	16	17
1000	nil α=.05	3.84	3.00	2.61	2.38	2.22	2.11	2.02	1.95	1.89	1.84	1.76	1.67	1.58	1.47	1.40	1.33	1.24
	nil α=.01	6.66	4.63	3.80	3.34	3.04	2.82	2.66	2.53	2.42	2.34	2.20	2.06	1.90	1.71	1.61	1.49	1.35
	pow .5	3.79	2.46	1.87	1.51	1.37	1.20	1.07	0.97	0.96	0.89	0.77	0.71	0.55	0.48	0.41	0.30	0.23
	pow .8	7.81	4.81	3.61	2.94	2.55	2.24	2.02	1.84	1.72	1.60	1.41	1.23	1.01	0.80	0.67	0.52	0.36
	1% α=.05	23.25	12.26	8.59	6.76	5.66	4.93	4.40	3.99	3.66	3.42	3.05	2.68	2.30	1.93	1.74	1.54	1.34
	1% α=.01	30.44	15.89	11.01	8.59	7.13	6.16	5.47	4.95	4.54	4.22	3.73	3.24	2.75	2.25	2.00	1.74	1.46
	pow .5	22.91	11.53	7.73	5.83	4.68	3.92	3.37	3.08	2.73	2.47	2.07	1.67	1.33	0.95	0.72	0.54	0.33
	pow .8	31.72	16.01	10.78	8.16	6.58	5.53	4.78	4.27	3.81	3.45	2.91	2.38	1.86	1.33	1.04	0.76	0.47
	5% α=.05	78.99	40.07	27.09	20.61	16.71	14.12	12.27	10.88	9.79	8.93	7.63	6.32	5.00	3.71	3.06	2.41	1.75
	5% α=.01	92.43	46.81	31.60	23.96	19.41	16.37	14.20	12.57	11.30	10.29	8.77	7.25	5.73	4.21	3.45	2.68	1.92
	pow .5	78.54	39.29	26.20	19.66	15.74	13.12	11.25	9.85	8.75	7.88	6.57	5.36	4.02	2.69	2.06	1.40	0.75
	pow .8	93.82	46.97	31.35	23.54	18.86	15.73	13.50	11.83	10.53	9.48	7.92	6.42	4.83	3.25	2.49	1.70	0.92
10000	nil α=.05	3.84	3.00	2.61	2.37	2.21	2.10	2.01	1.94	1.88	1.83	1.75	1.66	1.57	1.46	1.39	1.32	1.22
	nil α=.01	6.64	4.61	3.78	3.32	3.02	2.80	2.64	2.51	2.41	2.32	2.19	2.04	1.88	1.70	1.59	1.47	1.33
	pow .5	3.79	2.34	1.86	1.51	1.37	1.20	1.07	0.96	0.87	0.84	0.77	0.63	0.55	0.43	0.36	0.30	0.22
	pow .8	7.81	4.76	3.60	2.93	2.54	2.23	2.00	1.83	1.68	1.59	1.40	1.20	1.00	0.77	0.64	0.51	0.34
	1% α=.05	135.8	68.43	45.99	34.77	28.04	23.55	20.34	17.94	16.07	14.57	12.33	10.06	7.80	5.56	4.44	3.31	2.19
	1% α=.01	152.7	76.89	51.63	38.99	31.39	26.35	22.74	20.04	17.94	16.26	13.73	11.21	8.69	6.16	4.90	3.63	2.36
	pow .5	134.7	67.36	44.90	33.68	26.95	22.46	19.25	16.85	14.98	13.48	11.23	8.99	6.74	4.55	3.41	2.31	1.19
	pow .8	154.1	77.06	51.39	38.56	30.86	25.73	22.06	19.31	17.17	15.46	12.90	10.32	7.75	5.22	3.93	2.66	1.37
	5% α=.05	601.3	301.2	213.3	151.1	121.1	101.1	86.81	76.09	67.76	61.09	51.08	41.08	31.07	21.06	16.05	11.04	6.03
	5% α=.01	637.8	319.4	213.2	160.3	128.4	107.2	92.03	80.66	71.81	64.74	54.12	43.51	32.89	22.28	16.97	11.67	6.36
	pow .5	600.6	300.3	200.1	150.1	120.1	100.1	85.79	75.05	66.72	60.06	50.04	40.02	30.01	20.01	15.01	10.04	5.03
	pow .8	639.9	319.5	213.1	159.9	127.7	106.6	91.23	79.99	71.07	64.00	53.31	42.68	31.94	21.33	16.00	10.68	5.38

Hyp - hypothesis being tested: nil = traditional null; 1% = treatments account for 1% or less of the variance; 5% = reatments account for 5% or less of the variance in outcomes

F for - F values provided for alpha levels of .05 and .01; for traditional null (nil) and minimum-effect (1% and 5%) null hypotheses.
F-equivalent values needed for power of .50 and power of .80 (with α=.05) to reject that hypothesis are also provided

References

Algina, J., & Keselman, H. J. (1997). Detecting repeated measures effects with univariate and multivariate statistics. *Psychological Methods, 2*, 208–218.

Bunce, D., & West, M. A. (1995). Self perceptions and perceptions of group climate as predictors of individual innovation at work. *Applied Psychology: An International Review, 44*, 199–215.

Carroll, J. B. (1993). *Human cognitive abilities: A survey of factor-analytic studies.* Cambridge, England: Cambridge University Press.

Cascio, W. F., & Zedeck, S. (1983). Open a new window in rational research planning: Adjust alpha to maximize statistical power. *Personnel Psychology, 36*, 517–526.

Chow, S. L. (1988). Significance test or effect size? *Psychological Bulletin, 103*, 105–110.

Clapp, J. F., & Rizk, K. H. (1992). Effect of recreational exercise on midtrimester placental growth. *American Journal of Obstetrics and Gynecology, 167*, 1518–1521.

Cohen, J. (1962). The statistical power of abnormal-social psychological research. *Journal of Abnormal and Social Psychology, 65*, 145–153.

Cohen, J. (1988). *Statistical power analysis for the behavioral sciences* (2nd ed.). Hillsdale, NJ: Lawrence Erlbaum Associates.

Cohen, J. (1994). The earth is round ($p < .05$). *American Psychologist, 49*, 997–1003.

Cohen, J., & Cohen, P. (1983). *Applied multiple regression/correlation analysis for the behavioral sciences.* Hillsdale, NJ: Lawrence Erlbaum Associates.

Cortina, J. M., & Dunlap, W. P. (1997). On the logic and purpose of significance testing. *Psychological Methods, 2*, 161–173.

Cotton, M. M., & Evans, K. M. (1990). An evaluation of the Irlen lenses as a treatment for specific reading disorders. *Australian Journal of Psychology, 42*, 1–12.

Cowles, M. (1989). *Statistics in psychology: An historical perspective.* Hillsdale, NJ: Lawrence Erlbaum Associates.

Cowles, M., & Davis, C. (1982). On the origins of the .05 level of statistical significance. *American Psychologist, 37*, 553–558.

Evans, B. J., & Drasdo, N. (1991). Tinted lenses and related therapies for learning disabilities: A review. *Ophthalmic and Physiological Optics, 11*, 206–217.

Fick, P. L. (1995). Accepting the null hypothesis. *Memory and Cognition, 23*, 132–138.

Greenhouse, S. W., & Geisser, S. (1959). On method in the analysis of profile data. *Psychometrika, 24*, 95–112.

Greenwald, A. G. (1993). Consequences of prejudice against the null hypothesis. In G. Keren & C. Lewis (Eds.), *A handbook for data analysis in the behavioral sciences: Methodological issues* (pp. 419–448). Hillsdale, NJ: Lawrence Erlbaum Associates.

Grissom, R. J. (1994). Probability of the superior outcome of one treatment over another. *Journal of Applied Psychology, 79*, 314–316.

Haase, R. F., Waechter, D. M., & Solomon, G. S. (1982). How significant is a significant difference? Average effect size of research in counseling psychology. *Journal of Counseling Psychology, 29*, 58–65.

Hagen, R. L. (1997). In praise of the null hypothesis statistical test. *American Pychologist, 52*, 15–24.

Hedges, L. V. (1987). How hard is hard science, how soft is soft science? *American Psychologist, 42*, 443–455.

Himel, H. N., Liberati, A., Gelber, R. D., & Chalmers, T. C. (1986). Adjuvant chemotherapy for breast cancer: A pooled estimate based on published randomized control trials. *Journal of the American Medical Association, 256*, 1148–1159.

Horton, R. L. (1978). *The general linear model: Data analysis in the social and behavioral sciences.* New York: McGraw-Hill.

Hunter, J. E., & Hunter, R. F. (1984) Validity and utility of alternative predictors of job performance. *Psychological Bulletin, 96*, 72–98.

Hunter, J. E., & Hirsh, H. R. (1987). Applications of meta-analysis. In C. L. Cooper and I. T. Robertson (Eds.), *International review of industrial and organizational psychology.* (pp. 321–357). Chichester, England: Wiley.

Hunter, J. E., & Schmidt, F. L. (1990). *Methods of meta-analysis: Correcting error and bias in research findings.* Newbury Park, CA: Sage.

Irlen, H. (1993, August). *Scotopic sensitivity and reading disability.* Paper presented at the 91st Annual Convention of the American Psychological Association, Anaheim, CA.

Kraemer, H. C., & Thiemann, S. (1987). *How many subjects?* Newbury Park, CA: Sage.

Landy, F. J., Farr, J. L., & Jacobs, R. R. (1982). Utility concepts in performance measurement. *Organizational Behavior and Human Performance, 30*, 15–40.

Lipsey, M. W. (1990). Design sensitivity. Newbury Park, CA: Sage.

Lipsey, M. W., & Wilson, D. B. (1993). The efficacy of psychological, educational, and behavioral treatment. *American Psychologist, 48*, 1181–1209.

Martin, F., Mackenzie, B., Lovegrove, W., & McNicol, D. (1993). Irlen lenses in the treatment of specific reading disability: An evaluation of outcomes and processes. *Australian Journal of Psychology, 45*, 141–150.

McDaniel, M. A. (1988). Does pre-employment drug use predict on-the-job suitability? *Personnel Psychology, 41*, 717–729.

Meehl, P. (1978). Theoretical risks and tabular asterisks: Sir Karl, Sir Ronald, and the slow progress of psychology. *Journal of Consulting and Clinical Psychology, 46*, 806–834.

Morrison, D. E. & Henkel, R. E. (1970). *The significance test controversy: A reader.* Chicago: Aldine.

Murphy, K. (1990). If the null hypothesis is impossible, why test it? *American Psychologist, 45*, 403–404.

Murphy, K., & Myors, B. (1997). *Tests of minimum-effect hypotheses in the general linear model.* Manuscript submitted for publication.

Nagel, S. S. & Neff, M. (1977). Determining an optimal level of statistical significance. *Evaluation Studies Review Annual, 2*, 146–158.

Neale, M. B. (1973). *The Neale analysis of reading ability.* London: Macmillan.

Patnaik, P. B. (1949). The non-central $c2$- and F distributions and their applications. *Biometrika, 36*, 202–232.

Rosenthal, R. (1991). *Meta-analytic procedures for social research.* Newbury Park, CA: Sage.

Rosenthal, R. (1993). Cumulating evidence. In G. Keren & C. Lewis (Eds.), *A handbook for data analysis in the behavioral sciences: Methodological issues* (pp. 519–559). Hillsdale, NJ: Lawrence Erlbaum Associates.

Rouanet, H. (1996). Bayesian methods for assessing the importance of effects. *Psychological Bulletin, 119*, 149–158.

Schmidt, F. L. (1992). What do the data really mean? Research findings, meta-analysis and cumulative knowledge in psychology. *American Psychologist, 47*, 1173–1181.

Schmidt, F. L. (1996). Statistical significance testing and cumulative knowledge in psychology: Implications for training of researchers. *Psychological Methods, 1,* 115–129.

Schmidt, F. L., Hunter, J. E., McKenzie, R. C., & Muldrow, T. W. (1979). Impact of valid selection procedures on work-force productivity. *Journal of Applied Psychology, 71,* 432–439.

Schmidt, F. L., Mack, M. J., & Hunter, J. E. (1984). Selection utility in the occupation of U.S. park ranger for three modes of test use. *Journal of Applied Psychology, 69,* 490–497.

Schmitt, N., Gooding, R. Z., Noe, R. D., & Kirsch, M. (1984). Metaanalyses of validity studies published between 1964 and 1982 and the investigation of study characteristics. *Personnel Psychology, 37,* 407–422.

Sedlmeier, P., & Gigerenzer, G. (1989). Do studies of statistical power have an effect on the power of studies? *Psychological Bulletin, 105,* 309–316.

Serlin, R. A., & Lapsley, D. K. (1985). Rationality in psychological research: The good-enough principle. *American Psychologist, 40,* 73–83.

Serlin, R. A., & Lapsley, D. K. (1993). Rational appraisal of psychological research and the good-enough principle. In G. Keren & C. Lewis (Eds.), *A handbook for data analysis in the behavioral sciences: Methodological issues* (pp. 199–228). Hillsdale, NJ: Lawrence Erlbaum Associates.

Siegel, S. (1956). *Nonparametric statistics for the behavioral sciences.* New York: McGraw-Hill.

Tatsuoka, M. (1993a). Effect size. In G. Keren & C. Lewis (Eds.), *A handbook for data analysis in the behavioral sciences: Methodological issues* (pp. 461–179). Hillsdale, NJ: Lawrence Erlbaum Associates.

Tatsuoka, M. (1993b). Elements of the general linear model. In G. Keren & C. Lewis (Eds.), *A handbook for data analysis in the behavioral sciences: Statistical issues* (pp. 3–42). Hillsdale, NJ: Lawrence Erlbaum Associates.

Tiku, M. L., & Yip, D. Y. N. (1978). A four-moment approximation based on the *F* distribution. *Australian Journal of Statistics, 20*(3), 257–261.

Wilcox, R. R. (1992). Why can methods for comparing means have relatively low power, and what can you do to correct the problem? *Current Directions in Psychological Science, 1,* 101–105.

Winter, S. (1987). Irlen lenses: An appraisal. *Australian Educational and Developmental Psychologist, 4,* 1–5.

Yuen, K. K. (1974). The two-sample trimmed *t* for unequal population variances. *Biometrika, 61,* 165–170.

Zimmerman, D. W., & Zumbo, B. D. (1993). The relative power of parametric and nonparametric statistical methods. In G. Keren & C. Lewis (Eds.), *A handbook for data analysis in the behavioral sciences: Methodological issues* (pp. 481–518). Hillsdale, NJ: Lawrence Erlbaum Associates.

Zwick, R., & Marascuilo, L. A. (1984). Selection of pairwise comparison procedures for parametric and nonparametric analysis of variance models. *Psychological Bulletin, 95,* 148–155.

Author Index

Subject Index